NEW ZEALAND

PUBS

MW00981636

NEW ZEALAND

PUBS

175 CLASSIC
PUBS TO VISIT

NEW
HOLLAND

PETER JANSSEN

CONTENTS

INTRODUCTION

In 1894 New Zealand had 1,719 licensed premises serving a population of well under one million. Most of the old hotels have long gone, either burnt down or demolished, especially in the cities. This book is a guide to the 175 of the best historic pubs left today. The criteria for this book was simple to be considered, a pub had to have been built as a pub before 1967 (the end of six o'clock closing) and still be operating as a pub today. Therefore, modern bars and newer pubs occupying buildings such as an old post office or bank are not included. Another consideration was that the pub have something to offer the modern traveller in terms of atmosphere, food or accommodation.

Historical information has presented many challenges. Licenses and names changed regularly, and pubs were burnt down, shifted or washed away; making accurate information very hard to establish. Publicans often had little or no knowledge of their pubs, and in many cases were completely misinformed. Moreover, the pub is the original home of the tall tale and without a doubt many of these tales have been retold in this book. In the true spirit of the New Zealand pub, truth has not stood in the way of a good story. However, the book tries to be as accurate as possible in the face of often conflicting information from apparently reliable sources, and it would be good to hear from anyone who can provide more precise information about the pubs included in this book. Those hotels that are registered as listed buildings by New Zealand Heritage are indicated as such, along with the category, either one or two.

Food and accommodation are tricky things to measure in a guide book. Hotels have accommodation ranging from smart rooms with en suites right down to backpacker bunk rooms, campervan sites and camping grounds. Rather than have a complicated pricing system, this book gives just a short description of what is available and relies on travellers either using the websites or phoning ahead. That said, the hotels in this book have better-than-average hotel rooms, though shared facilities are still very common, which for the budget-minded traveller often offers exceptional value.

Pub food was a bit more straightforward, but it also varies considerably, from gastro pubs down to a simple burger menu. Menus have been described in general terms rather than detail.

For ease of travel the pubs are usually listed from north to south within 13 regions. An alphabetical index is provided to find any individual pub by name.

NORTH

ISLAND

NORTHLAND

WAIPAPAKAURI HOTEL

1108 Far North Road/SH1, Waipapakauri
Ph: 09 406 7408
Web: www.waipapakaurihotel.co.nz
Built: 1917
Heritage category 2
Food: Classic pub food, you won't go hungry here.
Accommodation: Mixture of en suite bedrooms, shared
facilities and backpacker accommodation.

Established in the late nineteenth century, the original hotel, called the Traveller's Rest, burnt down in 1916. It was replaced in 1917 with the pub that stands today.

During WWII the New Zealand Air Force established its most northerly airfield adjacent to the pub, and from here planes refuelled and left the country to go overseas. The air force requisitioned the hotel for its own use and even used part of the pub as a hospital, with the nurse's quarters now the backpackers accommodation. A plaque inside the hotel is in recognition of the pub's war efforts, which along with photographs and memorabilia makes the Waipapakauri an essential stop for aviation and military buffs. A monument to the air force, in the form of a propeller, is right next door.

Recently renovated, the hotel makes the most of its history, with the original timber flooring exposed and historic photographs and newspaper clippings in the comfortable bar and dining area that runs along the front of the hotel. Out the back things are very different. A small bar celebrating Americana opens out into a large garden bar complete with a stage that hosts regular live music events.

MANGONUI HOTEL

112 Waterfront Road, Mangonui
Ph: 09 406 0003
Web: www.mangonuihotel.co.nz
Built: 1905
Heritage category 1
Food: Roast dinners are available at the bar, while at one end of the building simpler meals are offered, with fresh seafood a specialty.
Accommodation: A range of upstairs rooms are available, from double rooms with en suites through to backpackers. Most rooms have views of the harbour from the veranda.

This fine Edwardian building opened in 1905 and has as neighbours several other historic buildings constructed around the same period: the Court House (1896), the Post Office (1904) and the General Store (1907). Largely unchanged, the broad verandas and old sash windows give a grand view over Mangonui harbour and its small port, busy with both pleasure boats and commercial fishing boats trying their luck in waters renowned for excellent fishing.

A single large bar with huge windows overlooking the harbour, this is a friendly and welcoming spot for both locals and visitors, and it opens on to a spacious outdoor area that is very popular in summer. The walls are packed with nautical and historical photos and memorabilia, along with hunting and fishing trophies. The star attraction is Barney, a sulfur-crested cockatoo. Well over 40 years old, Barney is completely at home in the hectic pub environment, having started his life in the Taheke Tavern near Kaikohe before taking up residence in the Mangonui Hotel. Particularly popular with children, Barney thrives on the attention; though he is not shy of taking the odd nip of a customer now and then.

OLD OAK INN

68 Waterfront Road, Mangonui
Ph: 09 406 0665
Web: www.oldoakinn.co.nz
Built: 1861
Food: An Indian restaurant, the Indian Spice, is in an historic building adjoining the main hotel.
Accommodation: The boutique hotel features six individually designed en suite rooms.

Complicated hotel histories are not unusual in New Zealand, but the story of the Old Oak is in a league of its own.

Although Mangonui is an old whaling station dating back to the 1830s, the area was without a hotel until Scotsman John McIntosh built the Mangonui Hotel in 1861 (later to become the Old Oak). However, an earlier pub, oddly called the Donneybrook Hotel, did exist at Mill Bay on the other side of the harbour. In 1905 the then proprietor, John Bray of the Mangonui, built another hotel and transferred the name and the license to the new hotel. The old hotel then obtained the license and name of the old Donneybrook Hotel, which had in the meantime changed its name to the Settlers Hotel and had gone out of business. Not long after, the hotel changed its name yet again to the Old Oak, a name it retains today (an oak was planted on the site in the 1870s). The verandas were added in 1910, but in 1918 authorities decided that Mangonui should only have one hotel, so the Old Oak became in turn a private residence, a butcher's shop and then a boarding house. In the 1940s and 50s the hotel was used as a foster home by the Blucher family and at one point accommodated 18 foster children at the same time. Mr Bulcher, needing a space to fix his Morris Minor, took a chainsaw to one of the walls and cut a hole big enough to get the car inside the room. Today French doors fill the hole.

During the 1980s the Old Oak reverted to a hotel and today is one of New Zealand's most attractive small hotels. Located right on the waterfront overlooking the harbour, the Old Oak now only provides accommodation. The stylish and comfortable rooms are all individually decorated. The garden is designed in the original colonial style.

The original old oak died after being hit by a tour bus and today a much younger tree is thriving in front of the hotel. While you are there, ask to see the Smugglers Cave behind the hotel, a genuine hideaway used both for storing contraband to avoid duty and to hide seaman who had jumped whaling ships.

MARLIN HOTEL

Whangaroa Road, Whangaroa
Ph: 09 405 0347
Web: www.marlinhotel.co.nz
Built: Around 1920
Food: Good pub meals in a building adjoining the hotel.
Accommodation: Rooms with en suites, some with views over the harbour.

Little is known about the history of the Marlin Hotel, though the current building dates from around 1920 when it replaced an earlier hotel that likely burnt down. Since then the Marlin has undergone several facelifts over the years but still retains the handsome 1920s façade overlooking the Whangaroa Harbour. In 2002 the Marlin narrowly survived a fire, graphically demonstrating that fire is still a major threat to New Zealand's old wooden hotels.

Whangaroa Harbour attracted early attention from Europeans, not only for its fine sheltered anchorage, but also for the kauri that was ideal for the spars of sailing ships. In 1809 a confrontation with local Maori and the crew of the *Boyd* ended disastrously, with the ship being burnt and the 66 crew members, including the captain, being killed. Today the wreck of the *Boyd* lies off Red Island in the harbour. In the 1920s the harbour became known as a base for big game fishermen, including the famous American author Zane Grey.

Huge windows along the north side of the Marlin's main bar overlook the harbour and the wharf, and the walls are lined with photos of marlin caught off the coast from Whangaroa based boats. The dining area has doors that fold right back, allowing uninterrupted views of the harbour, and adjoining is a wonderful sheltered outdoor area ideal for casual summer drinking and eating.

DUKE OF MARLBOROUGH

35 The Strand, Russell
Ph: 09 403 7829
Web: www.theduke.co.nz
Built: 1920s
Food: The main restaurant is elegant evening dining overlooking the bay and specialising in fresh seafood. The Bistro, open for lunch and dinner, serves lighter meals.
Accommodation: 26 rooms range from waterfront luxury to standard rooms. All rooms are en suite and a waterfront bungalow is also available.

New Zealand's oldest licensed hotel, the Duke of Marlborough holds the No.1 License issued by the Colonial Treasury on 14 July 1840; though a hotel was built on the site by John Johnston in 1827. At that time Russell was known as Kororareka and operated as New Zealand's first capital for a short nine month period in 1840, but in reality it was wild, rough town better known as 'the hell hole of the Pacific.' The first hotel burnt down after Hone Heke captured and sacked the town in 1845, forcing the European population to flee to Auckland, which had not long since become the new capital of the fledging colony. The Duke was rebuilt, though Russell never recovered from the raid and remained a quaint backwater settlement. Burnt down in 1875, the Duke was again rebuilt, only to burn down yet again in the 1920s when the boarding house next door caught fire. The building standing today is believed to be a boarding house that was transported by barge from another island in the bay. The Duke of Marlborough is the only survivor of the nine hotels that operated in Russell in the nineteenth century.

A destination in its own right, the Duke today combines history with all the modern comforts and is popular for both accommodation and dining. Open verandas overlook the sea, while inside rich decoration, polished wood and elegant furniture creates a gracious atmosphere fittingly appropriate to this historic town. The ferries from Paihia run very regularly both during the day and evening, making this an ideal dining destination at any time of the year.

HOREKE HOTEL

2118 Horeke Road, Horeke, Hokianga
Ph: 09 401 9133
Built: Around 1833
Food: Typical pub fare but also a blackboard menu in the
restaurant, using fresh local produce when available.
Accommodation: Attractive double rooms, all en suite and overlooking the
water; including a honeymoon suite, plus a nearby house that sleeps four.

The Horeke Hotel in the upper Hokianga Harbour is not only the oldest pub building in New Zealand, but also one of the country's oldest European buildings. When the pub was first established is uncertain, but it is believed that a building operating as a pub was in existence by 1826, supplying liquor to the workers at the local shipbuilder's yard – the first commercial shipbuilding operation in New Zealand. The hip-gabled hotel was built about 1833 and considerably extended and altered since. Just how much of the first pub stands is debatable, though the pit sawn kauri floors which have some boards still attached with handmade nails are definitely original.

Horeke boasts several New Zealand firsts. Jackie Marmon, or Cannibal Jack – believed to be the first white person to settle in the Hokianga – helped build the hotel, and in 1837, Horeke was the site of New Zealand's first judicial execution when a Maori slave was shot on the small island in the front of the hotel for his part in the murder of Harry Biddle. It was also at Horeke that the colourful Baron Charles de Thierry arrived to set up a personal fiefdom in the Hokianga, after having met Hongi Hika in Britain in 1829 and, according to De Thierry, had purchased 40,000 acres from Hongi for the price of 36 axes. In 1840 the hotel was the site of the country's first post office after a petition from the locals convinced Governor Hobson to set up a service between the Bay of Islands and Horeke. At nearby Mangungu Mission House (built in 1838-39) many of the Hokianga chiefs attended the third signing of the Treaty of Waitangi on 12 February 1840, and the following day Governor Hobson provided a feast for the chiefs – quite likely the first government sponsored hui in New Zealand. Photographs show the hotel was extended in 1882 to accommodate passengers on the Penny Coaches that ran from the Bay of Islands to Horeke, and extended again sometime later. Though it had been operating for more than 15 years, the Horeke wasn't actually licensed until 1842.

Just as it did in 1833, the Horeke Hotel sits right on the water, and with the wharf right out front it is still accessible by boat. The two bars both open out onto a wide wooden deck and beyond that a wide sweep of lawn, the perfect spot on a warm summer's day. A beautifully carved pou (pole), the work of a local Maori craftsman, is the centrepiece of the main bar. The extensive use of native timbers give the bars a warm, inviting ambience. One bar top is made of wooden slabs from New Zealand's first Norfolk pine, complete with an embedded musket ball (presumably the tree was the backstop to target practice). Only a little bit off the beaten track, at the Horeke the atmosphere is warm and friendly, the food tasty and the beds clean and comfortable, so make the effort and make the trip. The pub is an ideal base for those doing the Twin Coast Cycleway that runs from Paihia to Mangungu on the Hokianga Harbour, just three kilometres from Horeke.

TOWAI TAVERN

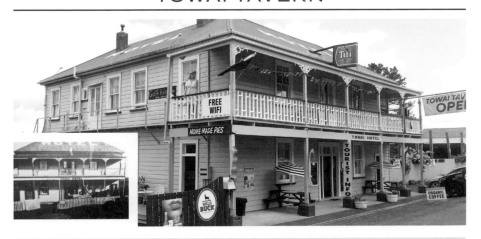

SH 1, Towai
Ph: 09 433 4900
Web: towaihotel@xtra.co.nz
Built: 1872
Heritage category 2
Food: Good country cooking using local and organic produce.

Built in 1872 down the hill by the railway, 60 years later (in 1932) the hotel was hauled up the hill to sit alongside the main road, with the help of a Cat 60 that is still operational and is now in the Matakohe Museum. Though the move took three days, the pub opened every evening to serve drinks.

Completely renovated in late 2007, the restoration of the Towai was undertaken with great attention to detail; from restoring the old sash windows, to replicating the original doors, and even matching the lettering on the pub to that in a photo taken in the opening years of the twentieth century. Even the old fireplace is back in action, and great place to kick back on the sofa and toast your feet. The bar top is a huge, spectacular piece of swamp kauri. Throughout the pub are whimsical touches such as the mannequins on the upstairs veranda, the vintage vinyl records and covers in the ladies' toilet and the outdoor bar created from an old concrete water tank.

Family run, the Towai is a great spot to stop on the trip north from Whangarei. Great pride is taken in providing meals sourced mainly from local, free range and organic produce and the menu features a variety of vegan and gluten options. Open early, the hotel offers breakfast, good coffee and homemade pies. On the northern, sunny side of the pub is a sheltered garden bar which hosts live music and features a single golf hole with a $1,000 prize for a hole in one.

KAMO HOTEL

567 Kamo Road, Kamo
Ph: 09 435 0011
Web: www.kamo.hotel
Built: 1937
Food: Hearty family meals.
Accommodation: Clean, tidy rooms, a mixture of en suite and shared facilities.

Now a quiet suburb of Whangarei, Kamo was once an important coach stop on the journey north, and around 1880 a hotel was built on the main road to accommodate travellers (old photographs of the coaching days are in the main foyer). In 1883 this hotel burnt down and was immediately replaced the following year. Rebuilt in 1905 as a much grander spa hotel, this building in turn burnt down in 1917, but it wasn't until 1936 that construction began on a new hotel. Opened in 1937, the architecture of the new brick and stucco building reflected an earlier era rather than the fashionable art moderne style that was all the rage at the time. The building still retains most of the original exterior features, while inside boasts a fine wooden staircase, dark wooden panelling and some stained-glass windows.

Occupying the corner is a spacious lounge bar and next door along the front of the building is the restaurant, which offers good value, family classic meals. The sports bar is enormous, and well known as the home of live music; top acts from New Zealand and Australia perform here regularly.

PARUA BAY TAVERN

1034 Whangarei Heads Road, Parua Bay
Ph: 09 436 5856
Web: www.paruabaytavern.co.nz
Built: 1937
Food: Gastro pub food plus stone-baked pizza.

The rather plain front of the Parua Bay Tavern doesn't prepare you for the treat when you step inside. The main bar completely opens out toward Whangarei Heads, to what is one of the best views of any pub in the country. Open doors, wide windows, and large decks face out over Parua Bay to Mt Manaia and over the harbour to Marsden Point and beyond. Beyond the terraces is a lovely grassy area leading down to their own wharf, and quite a few boaties make the trip across the water from Ruakaka for a quiet beer and a good meal.

An old wooden pub was originally built in the bay sometime in the 1880s, but details of the old hotel are somewhat murky and it appears to have been shifted once and burnt down at least once. What is clear is that fire destroyed the pub in 1937 and the pub, along with the license, moved into the dairy factory nearby. The jetty in front of the hotel was originally built to receive cream in cans from local farms. While the small rooms of the original pub have long gone, the wide-open bar and dining area retains a welcoming, friendly atmosphere, with warm colours and comfortable furnishings. Lined with historic photos, the walls are also decorated with fantastic posters from the 50s and 60s, advertising the pub.

Welcoming to visitors and families, the Parua is very much a local establishment and hosts numerous community events. On a warm summer's day there is no better place to be than at the Parua Bay Tavern, sitting on the wide deck or on the lawn, overlooking Whangarei Harbour.

PUBS AND FIRES

Fires were the scourge of early New Zealand hotels, especially those constructed of wood. With open fires for heating, candles and lamps for lighting and an iron range for cooking, it is a wonder that any old pubs survived. Most settlements didn't have a water supply, let alone a fire bridge, and once alight not much could be done to save the building. When the Marine Hotel (now the Prospect of Howick) burnt down in 1925 after someone left on an electric iron (a new invention at the time), Howick had neither a brigade nor a local water supply. In Timaru on 7 December 1868, fire destroyed the Royal Hotel along with 40 other buildings in the town. Subsequently a local bylaw made it a legal requirement for new buildings to be constructed of brick or stone. In Russell, when the Duke of Marlborough, New Zealand's oldest licensed pub, went up in flames, the local firemen were more intent on 'saving' the liquor than in fighting the fire.

South Islanders, however, are clearly more civic minded. When a fire broke out during at party at the Waipiata Hotel on Boxing Day 1932, revellers quickly became a bucket brigade, saving the hotel from burning down completely, though a boarder at the hotel died in the blaze. The Rutland Hotel in Whanganui succumbed to fire no less than four times. The Avoca just up the river burnt down, and then – just three days before the new hotel was to open in 1929 – it burnt down again.

Of course, modern pubs are not immune from fire, despite more sophisticated fire detection and professional fire fighting teams. The historic Spa Hotel in Taupo, dating back to the 1860s, burnt down in 1990, and the Marlin Hotel at Whangaroa in Northland narrowly escaped death by fire in 2002.

CENTRAL HOTEL

18 Victoria St, Dargaville
Ph: 09 439 8034
Web: www.centralhotel.biz
Built: 1901
Heritage category 2
Food: Good, honest pub meals.
Accommodation: Rooms with shared facilities upstairs.

The early history of this pub is uncertain. There is one story that tells of the Kaihu Hotel being established around 1818 on an adjacent site, and that would make this the oldest hotel premise in the country. Just when the old Kaihu Hotel was built is not really known, but what is known is that it was destroyed by fire, rebuilt on the present site in 1876 and at the same time changed its name to the Central Hotel. This hotel burnt down in 1901 and the building standing today dates from the same year. Located near the terminus of the railway line and having its own wharf, the hotel became a firm favourite with locals and travellers.

This heritage building is a fine, two-storey wooden hotel overlooking the Wairoa River, and is a friendly, unpretentious Kiwi pub. Even the resident ghost is well-behaved, being particularly fond of shutting doors and having a quiet nap; freshly made beds are found later to have the imprint of a body even though no one has used the room.

The comfortable main bar on the ground floor is airy and open, with views over to the river and the historic bandstand across the road. The local darts and pool clubs are based in the pub, and the long upstairs veranda is ideal spot to watch the world go by.

NORTHERN WAIROA HOTEL

Corner Victoria and Hokianga Roads, Dargaville
Ph: 09 439 8923
Built: 1878/1922
Heritage category 2
Food: Pub meals from lunch to dinner, served in a lovely, old-fashioned dining room.
Accommodation: 29 double, twin, single and family rooms with
both en suite and shared facilities to suit every budget.

Dominating the main intersection in Dargaville, the Northern Wairoa was constructed by Joseph Dargaville on the current site in 1878, and it is the town's grandest building. It has long been held that the hotel later burnt down and was rebuilt, but recent research shows that is not the case. In 1920 a kapok mattress upstairs caught fire and the local fire brigade saved the hotel by tossing the mattress out of the window into the street below. Already in need of renovation, the fire gave the owners the impetus to completely

upgrade the hotel, putting in six brick fire walls, cladding the exterior in brick, and at the same time significantly enlarging the hotel. It reopened in 1922.

With an exterior that has not changed since 1922, the large, sprawling hotel in the centre of Dargaville is hard to miss and today provides a sports bar, TAB and gaming room.

From the foyer, double doors lead to a wonderful and inviting traditional lounge, with high ceilings, dark wood panelling and comfortable seating arranged around a fire place. Adjoining the lounge is a spacious dining room that easily accommodates 100 people. The hotel is a popular destination for organisations such as car clubs, as it can cater for large groups. Like so many hotels, the Northern Wairoa has a resident ghost, a young girl around 10 years old who inhabits the upstairs bedroom.

KAIHU TAVERN

27 km north of Dargaville on SH 12
Ph: 09 439 0722
Built: 1892 – 1900
Heritage Category 2
Food: Simple menu of pub favourites that guarantee you don't leave hungry.

Confusion surrounds the early years of the Kaihu Hotel, north of Dargaville. It appears to have started life around 1892 as the Travellers Rest. Accommodating both travellers and boarders, but not selling alcohol the building was moved downhill to be closer to the new railway line which reached the area in 1896. Substantial additions in 1900 led to the owners applying for a liquor license as the Opanaki Hotel and despite fierce opposition from both temperance groups and the local Maori community, the license was granted later that year.

When the road through the kauri forest at Waipoua opened in 1928 the hotel became a popular stopping point for tourists. When the railway closed in 1959, the district became known as Kaihu, and in the late 1960s the hotel became the Kaihu Tavern.

The exterior is little changed since 1900 with the gabled roof of the original Travelers Rest still visible behind the later addition. A long public bar occupied most of the front section of the hotel, with a small ladies bar to the left where the bottle store is today.

Falling into decline, the hotel was rescued by the current owner and given a whole new lease of life. Keeping the best historical features such as the fireplace and leadlight windows, the main bar is spacious and pleasant with historical photos of the hotel and district lining the walls. The welcome is friendly and adjoining the main bar is an enormous covered outdoor area which acts as the unofficial club rooms of the Kaihu Rugby Club whose grounds are just over the road.

PAPAROA HOTEL

2039 Paparoa Valley Road/SH12, Paparoa
Ph: 09 431 7359
Web: www.paparoahotel.nz
Built: 1956
Food: Gastro pub with summer and winter menus that focus on strong and distinctive New Zealand flavours and seafood sourced from nearby Pahi.
Accommodation: Three bedrooms with shared facilities and one two-bedroom flat with bathroom.

Halfway between SH1 and Dargaville, the license for the Paparoa Hotel came from older pub at Pahi which closed down. Recently renovated, the Paparoa is today a very stylish hotel with a successful blend of mid-century and contemporary styles. Open, light and airy, the hotel has retained and accentuated its 1950s design with polished floors, the original cream-tiled fireplace and an exterior typical of the period. Alongside the pub is a welcoming garden bar. The food is definitely not the ordinary pub meals and it's complemented by an excellent wine list, but at the same time the local farmers and tradies feel right at home. This is also a place to stop for good coffee and a slice of homemade cake.

Just 6km from the superb Matakohe Kauri Museum, the hotel also has easy access to the newly established Paparoa Walk. Whether you are a local, from out of town or from across the seas, you will be welcome here.

MANGAWHAI TAVERN

Moir Street, Mangawhai
Ph: 09 431 4505
Web: www.mangawhaitavern.co.nz
Built: 1865
Heritage category 2
Food: Gourmet food with a focus on best food available and at reasonable prices. The menu is matched by an extensive wine list available by both the glass and the bottle.

Mangawhai today is a large and sprawling coastal settlement, but the early settlement was developed as a small river port where the tavern is situated today. The original pub was built in 1859, but burnt down just two years later and was replaced by the building still standing, though it underwent substantial renovations in 1905. One story tells of a local who rode his horse upstairs only to find that he couldn't get his horse back down again. The story unfortunately ends there, but as the horse is clearly not still in residence today it must have come back down somehow and at some time.

Retaining its Edwardian facade, the Mangawhai Tavern is a thoroughly modern pub and best known today for good music and good food. The location alongside the river is superb and the large garden bar, shaded by pohutukawas, overlooks the water. Dogs are welcome. The pub has been developed to accommodate live acts on both inside and outside stages, and it attracts some of New Zealand's best live music and a good crowd to match. In addition to the headline acts over the Christmas/New Year period, the Mangawhai Tavern also provides live entertainment every Friday night and Sunday afternoon, catering for a broad range of musical tastes. Complementing the historic nature of the pub, the walls of the main bar of the Mangawhai Tavern are lined with examples of contemporary New Zealand art work, which changes on a regular basis.

AUCKLAND
NORTH

THE BRIDGEHOUSE LODGE

16 Elizabeth St, Warkworth
Ph: 09 425 8351
Web: www.bridgehouse.co.nz
Built: 1930
Heritage category 2
Food: Extensive modern menu ranging from tasty snacks through to lighter meals and more substantial fare.
Accommodation: Fourteen rooms, all en suite.

Just when the first Bridgehouse was constructed and began operating as a hotel is unclear, however by 1859, local entrepreneur John Anderson Brown was living in the building with his housekeeper, Mrs Chandler, when the Bridgehouse became the local post office. Brown also built a flour mill and a bone mill for fertiliser, and an early alternative name for Warkworth was 'Brown's Mill'.

Later the building became an hotel, and around 1900 the original Bridgehouse was replaced by a larger building, which in turn was substantially altered in the 1930s. This structure, with its distinctive Tudor style, has largely remained unchanged since that time. Conference rooms and further accommodation was added in the 1980s.

Today the appeal of the Bridgehouse lies not so much in its historic ambience, but in the lovely restaurant and bar that sits above the Mahurangi River. Open and spacious, with its high ceilings, liberal use of timber and broad riverside terraces, this is the perfect spot to eat and drink in this pleasant town. Whether it is on a warm summer's evening or a cosy winter's night, the Bridgehouse's excellent food and attentive service is hard to beat.

THE ALBANY PUB

276 State Highway 17, Albany, Auckland
Ph: 09 415 9515
Built: 1936
Food: Excellent range of meals in a comfortable dining area.

Originally known as Lucas Creek, Albany township grew around the upper reaches of a small tidal river, where a small waterfall prevented boats from continuing upstream. The early settlement had a notorious reputation for illegal alcohol distilling and as a haven for characters of ill repute hiding out from the law. To distance themselves from this unsavoury reputation, the name changed to Albany in 1891 when the area became an important fruit growing district for the rapidly expanding Auckland city. The first hotel, the Wharfside Inn, is said to have been built around 1847 and was located just below the falls. The inn burnt down in 1886. Later that year William Stevenson rebuilt the pub as the Bridge Hotel, which was extensively renovated in 1890 and which in turn went up in flames in the early 1930s. The current hotel was built in 1936.

Once a popular stop on the busy road north of the city, the motorway now bypasses the old Albany settlement and today the Albany Pub is a very pleasant local pub. The main bar behind the hotel has extensive decks, perfect for a warm summer's evening or as a spot to enjoy the winter sun. Occupying the ground floor of the old pub, the dining area is more refined and is a pleasant spot for a quiet meal out or to celebrate a special occasion.

PUHOI PUB HOTEL

Corner Saleyards and Puhoi Roads, Puhoi
Ph: 09 422 0812
Web: www.puhoipub.com
Built: 1879
Heritage category 2
Food: The menu features good pub meals at very keen prices.

The German immigrants from Bohemia who settled in Puhoi certainly had their priorities right; first they built the pub and then the church. Although there was an older, more basic pub (oddly called the Baby Saloon) on the site, the current hotel was built in 1879 as the German Hotel, later changing the name to Puhoi Hotel when things Germanic fell way out of fashion during the First World War. Descendants of the original settlers still drink at the Puhoi, and occasionally the local Bohemian band plays at the pub. The single-storey building, which today is the main bar, is the oldest part of the Puhoi, with the two-storey section being built around the turn of the century.

Under the same family ownership since 1962, the Puhoi today is a very popular spot for both locals and visitors alike. Original features have been lovingly restored and the main entrance and dining room reflect an earlier and more gracious era. The main bar is packed with 'stuff', ranging from photos to newspaper cuttings, cartoons, bric-a-brac, international banknotes and just about anything else you can stick on a wall (or the ceiling). Out front the huge lawn, backed by a vine-covered gazebo and veranda, is a favourite destination for a drink on a Saturday summer afternoon; attracting large numbers of motorcyclists, whose gleaming machines line the road to the pub. The biggest event at the pub is the annual Woodchopping Carnival in January, though the opening day of shooting season also pulls in the crowds, with the day's bag of ducks lined up in front of the pub.

THE RIVERHEAD

68 Queen St, Riverhead
Ph: 09 412 8902
Web: www.theriverhead.co.nz
Built: 1876
Food: Excellent gastro pub with professional service. While
not extensive, the focus of the menu is on fresh and local,
complemented by an extensive wine list and craft beers.

Riverhead, on the northern reaches of the Waitematā Harbour, was once a busy river port; an important access to the Kaipara Harbour (and therefore to Northland) when travel by boat was considerably more convenient than travel by land. The first pub, known as the Forester's Arms (Riverhead was also a milling settlement), was built in 1843, not far from the existing pub. In 1856 the pub shifted, and then in 1876 was burnt down, to be replaced by the building there today. Later, Riverhead was the terminus for the railway line north, but in 1881 the railway line was extended from Kumeu to Auckland and Riverhead slowly became a quiet backwater.

While just a short drive from New Zealand's largest city, Riverhead still retains an unhurried atmosphere and, while the fortunes of the tavern have waxed and waned over the years, its location on the languid estuary of the Rangitopuni River is hard to beat. Now carefully renovated, this stylish gastro pub with wide shady terraces, overlooking the tree-lined river, is just magical, especially at high tide, and the place feels a million miles away from busy Auckland. The dodgy reputation of the large public bar is a distant memory and it is now a very relaxed family bar.

For those who have a boat the pub has its own wharf, though this part of the harbour is very tidal so you need to plan any boating trip carefully. It is also a very popular destination for kayak trips, but again a little planning around tides will make your paddle more enjoyable. If you are looking for a special place to take visitors, the Riverhead is just the spot.

THE NORTHCOTE TAVERN

37 Queen St, Northcote Point, Auckland
Ph: 09 480 7707
Web: www.northcotetavern.co.nz
Built: 1884
Food: The menu offers plenty of variety in a mixture of pub favourites and contemporary dishes, with something to please everyone, including the reasonable prices.

In 1840, Irishman Phillip Callan arrived in Auckland from Cork and purchased land just across the harbour at Stokes Point (later to become Northcote Point). Callan built a wharf and set up brickworks, the bricks from which he used to build a simple hotel in the late 1850s. The brick construction did not prevent the hotel from being destroyed by fire. Rising from the ashes, the new two-storey hotel, this time constructed from wood, was designed in the Italianate style and opened its doors in 1884.

Other than an extension in 1936, little has changed since 1884, and the hotel flourished as an essential stopping point for travellers on the ferries to and from the central city. Historic photos on the pub walls show Northcote Point in its heyday before the bridge, built in 1959, turned the point into a quiet backwater. No longer needing to service overnight travellers, the hotel became a tavern.

Oddly, for a pub so close to the city, the Northcote has the atmosphere of a country pub and is reminiscent (in a good way) of the 1960s. Very popular with locals, the main sports bar is packed after work with mainly men, talking the usual bloke nonsense, watching sport or just having a friendly beer. Visitors need to watch where they drink though; there is a special Punter's table for racing fans, and another for America's Cup fans. Some of the tables even carry memorial plaques to drinkers long since passed on. The tavern has long been a staunch supporter of New Zealand's America's Cup challenge and the large nautical flag pole out front dates from that time. The small lounge bar, called the Highland Bar, reflects the country of origin of the current owners and, recently redecorated, is resplendent in tartan carpet and other Scottish memorabilia.

Beyond the bars is a small dining area with the option of dining inside or out. In the old bottle store is a barista bar offering excellent coffee, opening at 9am most mornings and at 11am on Sunday.

THE ESPLANADE HOTEL

1 Victoria Road, Devonport, Auckland
Ph: 09 445 1291
Web: www.esplanadehotel.co.nz
Built: 1902
Heritage category 1

Food: Classic dishes with a contemporary touch, ranging from snacks and sharing platters through to larger meals, burgers and pizza. There is some thing for everyone here, including high tea and breakfast, all at prices that are surprisingly reasonable.

Accommodation: Sixteen boutique rooms, all en suite, plus a penthouse with two bedrooms, a living room and kitchen.

When the Esplanade Hotel opened in February 1903, Devonport was a thriving suburb; a short ferry ride from the central city, the start of the main road north and a popular destination for day trippers from Auckland. An older wooden hotel, the Flagstaff, had stood on the site since the 1880s. This was demolished to make way for a new building. Originally named the New Flagstaff, this was quickly changed to the Esplanade, a named that reflected the great British seaside resorts such as Brighton and Eastbourne.

At first glance, the architect Edward Bartley seemed an odd choice to design an hotel because he was better known for his religious buildings, which included St John's Church in Ponsonby, St David's Church on Symonds Street, Holy Trinity Church in Devonport, and the Synagogue. However, his elegant Edwardian Baroque hotel is a testament to his architectural versatility, and today the highly ornate Esplanade Hotel is one of Auckland's most treasured historic buildings, with little alteration over the years apart from the removal of several verandas.

The first publican, Edgar Horace White, advertised the Esplanade as a 'Modern Hotel furnished in the latest style', 'commanding a full view of the harbour' and suitable for 'Families, Tourists and the Travelling Public generally.'

Today the Esplanade successfully reflects the hotel's Edwardian origins with a stylish combination of historic and modern. Just inside the main entrance are two small conservatories, perfect for high tea or a heady cocktail, and beyond that an intimate bar to one side and a smart dining room to the other. The reception, at the foot of a period staircase, is graced by a chandelier. Wide open to the sea in summer, the main bar is full of light, enhanced by an open fire for those wet and chilly Auckland winter nights. Could there be more? How about a small ballroom, perfect for that intimate wedding or birthday party?

Outside there is oodles of seating on smart cane furniture, and the hotel's location just opposite the ferry wharf guarantees plenty of 'people watching'. On Saturday evenings the Esplanade hosts live jazz, so whether it is just for a coffee or for a night out, the short ferry ride across the harbour is well worth it.

AUCKLAND CITY

THE SHAKESPEARE HOTEL

61 Albert St, Auckland
Ph: 09 373 5396
Web: www.shakespearehotel.co.nz
Built: 1898
Heritage category 2
Food: The busy restaurant upstairs serves a good range of above-average pub food, though the service is indifferent.
Accommodation: Nine rooms upstairs, all en suite, and while not large, some have balconies and the location in downtown Auckland is hard to beat.

This fine, late Victorian hotel, built of distinct red brick imported from Melbourne, was commissioned by publican Thomas Foley, who was no stranger to the hotel industry. He was born in his parent's hotel in Wyndham Street, also named the Shakespeare, and later ran several taverns and hotels in Auckland, including the Star Hotel. Thomas was determined that his hotel would be the best, and a paper at the time commented 'The most carping critic would find it a difficult matter to place his finger on fault of the omission or commission.' In the 1960s and 70s, the upstairs piano bar was Auckland's best known gay pub, carefully watched over by the publican, the eagle-eyed Jessie Ray.

One of the few inner-city hotels to survive, the Shakespeare has been fortunate in having recent owners that have both retained and cherished the original character of the old pub. Along with the fine Victorian façade, interior features include kauri floors, old sash windows, period fireplaces and a fine wooden staircase. In places the walls have been stripped back to the original brick, and historic photos of old Auckland line the walls.

Yet there is much more. In 1986 Peter Barraclough set up one of New Zealand's first micro-breweries and, for beer aficionados, the Shakespeare is as well known for its ales as for its history. The brewery is actually located behind the Brewery Bar on the ground floor, with the stainless-steel vats visible behind the bar. Many of the beers on offer carry Shakespearian names such as *Falstaff's Real Ale* and *King Lear Old Ale*. The large bar/restaurant upstairs features a large veranda wrapping around the corner of the hotel, a very popular spot to survey the comings and goings along busy Albert Street.

HOTEL DEBRETT

Corner Shortland Street and High Street, Auckland
Ph: 09 925 9000
Web: www.hoteldebrett.com
Built: 1860/1925
Heritage category 2
Food: The menu is not extensive, but each dish is
carefully honed and beautifully prepared.
Accommodation: 25 luxury rooms, comfortable, stylish and superbly decorated.

A hotel has stood on this site since 1843 and was known as the Commercial Hotel until 1959 when it was renamed as Hotel De Brett and now, with a slight change to Hotel DeBrett.

In 1843 when this hotel was built, Shortland Street was the heart of the original settlement with the sea lapping the shore just below the hotel. Destroyed by fire in 1858, the wooden building was replaced by an impressive three storey brick hotel which remained largely unchanged until 1925.

In that year, the city decided to widen High Street by over 10 metres (High Street was then the width of the upper section of today's Vulcan Lane). The old hotel was pushed back four metres and was torn apart as an entire new hotel was built. Designed by Auckland architects Wade and Bartley, the new hotel was designed as a stylish Stripped Classical building, a forerunner of Art Deco and the exterior of the current hotel has changed very little since that time.

Further changes to the hotel came in the late 1950s, under the ownership of Dominion Breweries, the main entrance moved to High Street, the number of bedrooms, all with bathrooms was increased from 35 to 48 and the named changed to Hotel De Brett. The new Garden Bar introduced seated drinking, a revolutionary idea in an era when drinking was done standing up. However, a women's toilet on the ground floor wasn't installed until 1968. Under new ownership in 1984, the hotel had no fewer than five bars, despite the addition of ground-floor shops along High Street. In 1999 the elegant old hotel became a backpackers.

Ownership changed again in 2007 and with a major refurbishment, Hotel Debrett emerged as a stylish boutique hotel. The only remaining ground floor bar is the popular Cornerbar which with its folding windows and café style seating, is open to the street. Upstairs, the old courtyard has been transformed into an open light atrium which houses the restaurant and bar. There is a further small bar – styled to a hotel's bar from the nineteenth century. Many of the features of the 1925 hotel have been retained, especially the extensive wooden marquetry. Now a heritage listed building, the Hotel Debrett is set to be an integral part of Auckland city life for many years to come.

SIX O'CLOCK SWILL

With pubs closing at 6pm, patrons endeavoured to drink as much as possible prior to the last drinks call, and this became infamously known as 'the six o'clock swill'. Drinkers packed their tables with glasses and jugs of beer and drank at a furious pace before having to vacate the pub, an early version of 'binge drinking', which many see as having been invented by today's teenagers.

However, many publicans found a way around the law. Patrons could book a room for a night and then drink in the 'house bar', while at the Queen's Ferry in Auckland a secret back door was built in the back of the pub to allow those working on the wharves to continue drinking after hours. Country hotels, with minimal local policing, happily kept their own hours, and the West Coast of the South Island was particularly famous for ignoring the official closing times. When asked a question as to why their pubs were ignoring closing times, one West Coast publican commented 'I close at six and reopen at seven. Sharp!' and another replied indignantly 'Of course we have closing times, they are just a bit later than 6pm.'

THE OCCIDENTAL

6 - 8 Vulcan Lane, Auckland
Ph: 09 300 6226
Web: www.occidentalbar.co.nz
Built: 1870
Heritage category 1
Food: A broad menu that combines contemporary flavours with traditional tastes and includes Belgian dishes, several of which feature mussels. There are both Belgian and New Zealand beers on tap.

American sailor Edward Perkins had a reputation for being eccentric and entertaining, but when he opened the Occidental Hotel on 2 July 1870 he created one of the most innovative and stylish hotels of the day. Featuring a billiards and a reading room, imported wines and café style dining, The Occidental was famous for holding elaborate dinners, including celebrations for the Fourth of July. While the two parts of the hotel are in different styles, it is believed that they were built at much the same period and at a time when the lane was much narrower. The lower part of the lane was considerably widened in the 1920s, though the section of the lane above High Street remains today at the original width.

In 1999 the Occidental was totally renovated and emerged as Australasia's first Belgian bar, though original historical features have been retained and the exterior and ceilings are classified as historic. An overall musical theme runs through the Occidental and the warm interior colours were created to enhance this. Today the Occidental is a very popular eating spot, attracting a happy mix of retailers, officer workers and many tourists, and the tables outside are the ideal spot to watch the world go by.

THE EMPIRE HOTEL

137 Victoria Street West, Auckland
Ph: 09 373 4389
Web: www.empire.co.nz
Built: 1875
Food: A mixed range of food that includes classic, Asian and Mexican dishes along with pizza and small and large platters. Gourmet burgers are on offer in the Black Dog Burger Bar, and breakfast and cabinet food in the café.

When the Empire opened in 1875, Auckland was a town of just 15,000 people; but even at that stage it had over 90 hotels. The Empire was built by Edward Mahoney and Sons, who were also responsible for the Shakespeare, the Albion and the Birdcage. Located on a ridge between Freemans Bay and the town centre, the Empire catered for a working-class clientele, providing entertainment that included boxing matches and cockfights as well as ladies of dubious morals. Over the years the Empire remained a rowdy pub and even as late as the 1960s was favoured by Auckland's underworld. Times changed, and in the 1980s the run-down hotel was revived and became the city's leading gay pub. From there the Empire's fortunes have only looked up and now it is one of the city's most stylish and popular venues. Today the hotel retains its imposing Victoria façade and inside some elements of the old hotel remain, including exposed brickwork, the old staircase and polished kauri floors.

A popular weekday venue (closed Sundays), the Empire is a pub of many parts, catering for a diverse clientele. The main bar is sharply decorated in black and white, offering branded and craft beers, cocktails and a select wine list. Beyond the bar is a huge garden bar, mostly enclosed and easily accommodating large groups. On the corner is a small modern café that opens early for breakfast and offers excellent coffee. Alongside the main entrance is Black Dog Burgers, while upstairs is a small rooftop bar mainly for smokers. Street seating runs along the front of the building.

THE CAV

68 College Hill, Ponsonby, Auckland
Ph: 09 376 4230
Web: www.thecav.co.nz
Built: Around 1864
Food: Upmarket gastro pub with a stylish menu to match.

One of the few surviving wooden pubs in Auckland, the Cav (shortened from the Cavalier in 2014), then known as the Suffolk Hotel, was built sometime between 1864 and 1868. The exterior would still be recognisable to someone trudging up College Hill in the nineteenth century, and a photo taken in 1888 shows a familiar pub, but a radically different Auckland skyline. At that time Ponsonby was known as Dedwood, a name it retained until 1873. For most of its history the hotel was very much a local for working men. It is considered the home of Auckland Rugby League, as a meeting held on 6 April 1910 led to the formation of the first local Rugby League club.

After extensive renovations the Suffolk changed to the Cavalier Tavern in 1990, a name inspired by a large Belgian sandstone carving of a laughing Cavalier, a feature in the old bar.

More recently the pub has undergone a complete makeover and has emerged as a stylish gastro pub, very popular with locals. The extensive city-facing deck offers one of the best views of Auckland city of any restaurant or bar and is a great, cool spot late on a summer's afternoon to watch the sun go down over the city.

THE BIRDCAGE TAVERN

133 Franklin Rd, Freemans Bay, Auckland
Ph: 09 280 1690
Web: www.birdcage.co.nz
Built: 1886
Heritage category 2
Food: Contemporary menu, ranging from snacks to large platters catering for groups.

The Birdcage Tavern began life as the Rob Roy Hotel in 1886, designed by architects Edward Mahoney and Sons, who were also responsible for St Patrick's Cathedral and four other surviving Auckland hotels: the Occidental, the Albion, the Empire and the Shakespeare. At that time the Rob Roy was a waterfront hotel, and serviced the industrial area on the shores of Freeman's Bay and the working-class suburb that climbed the hills behind the bay.

Renamed the Birdcage Tavern in the early 1890s, the pub was purchased by NZTA in 2002 to extend the motorway. In order to accommodate the Victoria Park tunnel project, the entire hotel was moved 44 metres in 2009-2010. This massive undertaking used two hydraulic rams that moved the 750 tonne hotel 1.8 metres at a time along a purpose-built concrete track coated in Teflon. Once the tunnel work was completed, the hotel moved back to its original site in 2011-2012.

Though completely renovated inside, the pub takes advantage of its historical heritage. Sweeping across the front of the hotel, the combination bar/dining area occupies a wide crescent, with walls stripped back to the original brick and featuring an ornate Victorian fireplace and doorways. Outside is an expansive terrace, with umbrellas and seating overlooking Victoria Park; justifiably popular in the summer and on bright winter afternoons.

PITT ST PUB/NAVAL AND FAMILY HOTEL

Corner Karangahape Road and Pitt Street, Auckland
Ph: 09 222 0202
Web: pittstpub.co.nz
Built: 1895-1896
Heritage category 2
Food: Pub food with an inner-city touch, the 'bites' menu is more contemporary.

Occupying a prime site on Auckland's famous Karangahape Road (better known as just K Road), the Naval and Family Hotel opened in 1896 and was not the first pub on this site. An earlier hotel called the Naval was built by Patrick Darby in 1862 and was the first hotel on the road, though when the pub changed hands in 1867 several other hotels had sprung up along this busy highway. By 1882 the name had changed to the Naval and Family, and in 1894 fire destroyed the wooden hotel.

The new hotel was a grand affair. Three storeys high, it was typical of the late Victorian corner pub and the exterior has changed little over the last 120 years. Inside the hotel is another matter, with the configuration of the ground floor substantially altered in the 1930s. In the 1940s the verandas were added. During the 1960s the first floor became a lounge bar with accommodation on the top floor, but by 1972 the Naval and Family had become a tavern and in the 1990s the ground floor became a single space.

In more recent years, the hotel was home to Calendar Girls, a strip club which still occupies the first and second floors. But the good news is that ground floor is once again a pub, the smart Pitt St Pub. While the style is contemporary and stylish, and it is on K Road, this new addition to the history of this old hotel cleverly manages to create the relaxed atmosphere of a typical pub, even though it stays open to the early hours of the morning. If you are lucky, you might just grab the two tables on the footpath, the perfect spot to watch the colourful world of K Road go by.

Once the first hotel on K Road, the Naval and Family is now the last pub standing.

AUCKLAND EAST AND SOUTH

THE LANDING

2 Onehunga Harbour Road, Onehunga
Ph: 09 634 2544
Built: 1879
Food: Contemporary stylish menu with an appropriate emphasis
on seafood. The bar snacks are more typical pub fare and
the two course lunch special draws in the locals.

The Landing, previously known as the Manukau Hotel, is a familiar building to anyone driving to and from the Auckland airport, hugging the edge of the Manukau harbour at Onehunga. Sitting right above Onehunga Wharf, the pub today is marooned from Onehunga itself by the motorway, and is the only surviving pub from the heyday of Onehunga as an important port. Built in 1865 as the Manukau Hotel, fire destroyed the old building in 1879, but it was rebuilt immediately. The tram terminus from Auckland city was originally located opposite the hotel nearer the wharf, creating a centre of commercial activity, all of which has vanished.

As Onehunga declined and the area became more industrial, the Manukau Hotel followed the fortunes of the town. But luck held, and unlike all its rivals that have since disappeared, the Manukau was rescued and totally renovated in 2000. The old double fireplaces were uncovered and restored, the fabulous kauri floors now glow and shine and kauri timber from old outbuildings was used for the bar and tables.

Now renamed the Landing, the old pub had two public bars, a private bar, upstairs accommodation and a dining room, while today there is just a single bar and a dining room. Both are decorated in an appropriate nautical theme that works well with the Victorian style of the old hotel, and in the bar are several detailed historic photos of old Onehunga, including other local hotels long gone. Two ghosts, one a woman and the other a man, both dressed in Victorian clothing, haunt the first floor, but never venture downstairs.

While it is not the easiest place to get to from Onehunga, it is a little gem of old Auckland that is well worth the effort seeking out.

THE PROSPECT OF HOWICK/
THE GOOD HOME

Corner Picton Street and Uxbridge Road, Howick
Ph: 09 534 3199
Web: www.theprospect.co.nz
Built: 1928
Food: Smart dining offering light meals, coffee and more
substantial fare in a stylish restaurant, with indoor and outdoor
seating. A wide range of beers on tap and a good wine list.

Standing proudly in the main street of Howick, the Prospect is a fine old building that was renovated in 2006 and which artfully combines history with modern style. Known as the Marine Hotel, the first hotel was built of wood in 1906, attracting visitors from Auckland by both ferry and horse and described in 1908 as 'the large and well conducted house with views seaward and landward.' In 1925 the hotel burnt down, apparently due to that new invention, the electric iron, being left on. With no water supply or fire brigade, the hotel was totally incinerated. The new brick hotel was built by James Fletcher in 1928, and in 1934 it hosted the well-known British writer George Bernard Shaw, who commented at the time 'If I was beginning life I am not sure that I wouldn't start in New Zealand. I, being an old Victorian, am much more at home here than in London.' In 1977 the name changed from the Marine to the Prospect of Howick, reflecting Howick's past as Fencible settlement.

Today the Prospect cleverly divides in two. The Good Home bar and restaurant is smart and sophisticated, offering comfortable sofas for a chill drink and a modern menu, with stylish indoor décor and outdoor seating under an old plane tree for that warm summer day. Part of the dining area still retains the original plaster ceilings. Quite separate, behind the main building, the Bosun's Bar gaming room and sports bar offers plenty of screens for watching that big game, with an outdoor area that has a peep of the sea. The hotel regularly hosts live music events.

MURPHY'S LAW IRISH BAR

200 Great South Road, Drury, Auckland
Ph: 09 294 9054
Web: www.murphyslawirishbar.co.nz
Built: 1931
Food: Good, hearty and very filling pub meals.
Accommodation: Motorhome and caravan park behind the pub.

Little is known of the early history of the first hotel on this site, but it was likely built around 1860 to service both the British military camp and a local coal mine. Named the Railway Hotel, this pub went up in flames in 1927. Renamed the Jolly Farmer, the new hotel opened in 1931 and was constructed in a striking Tudor/arts and craft style which it still retains today. An old photo showing horses and hounds assembled in front of the pub for the local hunt could easily be mistaken as English. Located on the busy Great South Road, the pub was hugely popular as a stopping point for those travelling to and from the Waikato. The publicans were famous for working to their own rules, regularly ignoring the licensing laws of the day and providing an early morning tipple to passing truck drivers.

Now known as Murphy's Law Irish Bar, the extension of the Southern Motorway has bypassed this hotel, but it is well worth the short detour. Large and sprawling, with an enormous garden bar, you can fit an awful lot of people in here; there is a place for everyone in this comfy pub. British on the outside, the pub is just as British on the inside, retaining many of the of the original arts and craft features and accentuated by more recent décor. The result is an convivial atmosphere, making Murphy's Law a popular local pub and worth a visit by passing travellers.

THE KENTISH HOTEL

5 Queen Street Waiuku
Ph: 09 235 8367
Web: www.thekentishhotel.co.nz
Built: 1852
Heritage category 2
Food: The Kentish offers good value meals and the specialty of the house is fresh snapper.
Accommodation: Eleven good, clean rooms with shared facilities and access to the wide veranda that overlooks the street and river.

Like Riverhead on the northern reaches of the Waitematā Harbour, in the mid-nineteenth century Waiuku flourished as a portage town, providing a vital link between the Manukau Harbour and Onehunga to the important inland waterway of the Waikato River. The high hopes for a canal from the Manukau to the Waikato eventually faded, but even in later years a steamer travelled from Waiuku to Onehunga three times a week.

Overlooking the tidal Waiuku Inlet, the Kentish Hotel was built in 1852. Unusually for a wooden pub, it has neither changed its name nor has it been burnt down, though on occasions the flames came close. The builder and first publican was Edward Constable, who emigrated from Kent in England and took up land around Waiuku in 1851, immediately recognising the need for a hotel. While the hotel has been altered over the years, the two-storey hotel would still be recognisable to Mr Constable today. The hotel has been at the heart of Waiuku life since it was built, surviving the tense times during the land wars in the Waikato, and hosting visiting dignitaries such as the Maori King Te Wherowhero, Sir George Gray, Richard Seddon, Sir Joseph Ward and William Massey.

One of New Zealand's oldest pubs, the Kentish is a local favourite. Historic photos line the walls, the large bar is lively and friendly, and the dining area is a great place for a family night out. There is live music in the evenings from Thursday through to Saturday, and a garden bar area on the warm northern side of the building is just the spot for a quiet drink on summer's afternoon. Now into the second half of its second century, the Kentish is set to be the local favourite for some time yet.

Come in for
Coffee   High Tea   Royal Happy Hour

Breakfast   Lunch   Dinner

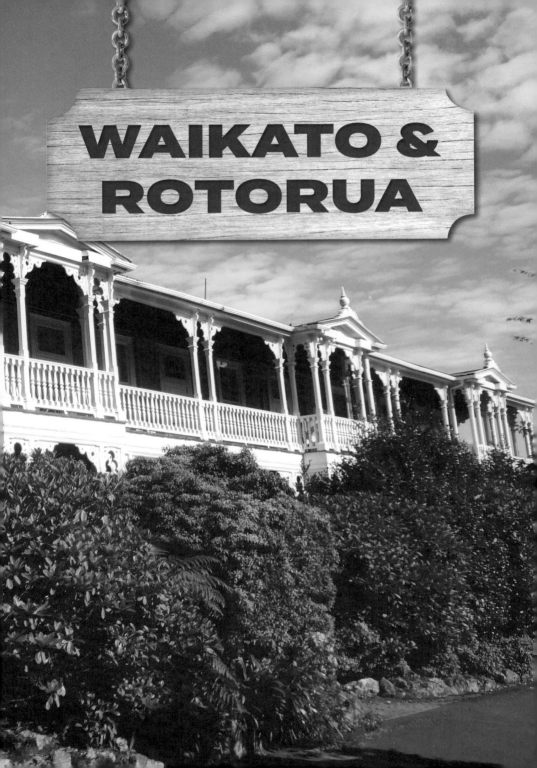

WAIKATO & ROTORUA

WAIKATO

BAY VIEW HOTEL

943 East Coast Road, Kaiaua
Ph: 09 232 2717
Built: 1953
Food: Good quality pub meals at excellent prices.

Stand in front of the Bay View Hotel, look up the hill behind and a bit to the right and you will notice an old house perched high above the Firth of Thames. This is the first hotel built at Kaiaua, in the late nineteenth century, and it was for accommodation only, with the bar in an adjoining tin shed. Later another hotel was constructed down on the flat, only to burn down and be replaced in 1953 by the low, sprawling building standing today.

You couldn't ask for a more pleasant Kiwi pub. Retaining many of its original mid-century features, the large main bar opens out to a huge garden bar, shaded by old trees and perfect for the kids to run around in without annoying anyone. Off the main entrance is the large, comfy dining room and historical photos, old newspapers and well-worn agricultural tools add to the welcoming atmosphere.

Located right next door to the legendary Kaiaua Fisheries, famous for their fish and chips, this hotel is the perfect spot, whether you are bird watching or soaking in the Miranda hot pools.

RANGIRIRI HOTEL

8 Talbot Street (just off SH 1), Rangiriri
Ph: 07 826 3467
Built: 1906
Food: Open for dinner and lunch, the hotel offers a good range
of pub food. But be warned: the Rangiriri is used to feeding
farmers and truckers, so make sure you come hungry.
Accommodation: Good clean rooms with shared facilities, kitchen and a lounge.

The original Rangiriri Hotel was built in 1866 on the low banks of the Waikato River, to service both the small township of Rangiriri (that once had a substantial eel factory) and travellers on the river, but frequent flooding forced a move away from the river to the present site. In 1904 the hotel was destroyed by fire and rebuilt in 1906 on the same site. The hotel retains the original exterior, including its fine old verandas, while the interior, modernised over the years, still has a traditional, warm atmosphere. In the dining room, keep an eye out for a solid old door that belongs to the old chiller room, that once kept the beer kegs cool. The huge palm tree in front of the hotel is believed to have been planted when the hotel was built. The main bar/dining room leads out to a long veranda overlooking a sunny garden. Alterations to the motorway now requires motorist to take a short detour off SH1 to the pub, and although a little down at heel, this fine old hotel is still worth a visit.

The hotel has a resident ghost, believed to be that of a woman who once lived in one of the front rooms upstairs. The ghost 'annoys' men (and only men) by locking doors, turning lights off and on, calling out names and interfering with the electrical systems. Some claim to have felt 'someone brushing past' when in fact there is no one there.

Opposite the hotel is the Rangiriri Historic Cemetery, containing graves and memorials to both the Maori defenders and British soldiers who died at the Battle of Rangiriri in 1863. It is fitting that the hotel has it own war memorial, though one much more recent. Private Leonard Manning, a popular local man, was killed while on border patrol near Suai in East Timor on 24 July 2000. At just 24 years old, he was the first New Zealand serviceman to be killed in action since 1971. The Rangiriri has a glass case containing photos and memorabilia of Leonard Manning.

NOTTINGHAM CASTLE HOTEL

Corner of Thames and Studholme Streets, Morrinsville
Ph: 07 889 5031
Heritage category 1
Built: 1914
Food: Great value pub meals in a very pleasant dining room.
Accommodation: Twenty-six clean and tidy rooms with
shared facilities and access to the verandas.

Affectionately known as the Nott, the Nottingham Castle is one of New Zealand's finest Edwardian hotels and it dominates the heart of Morrinsville.

Unplanned, Morrinsville began as a tiny settlement for Thomas Morrin's vast estate, Lockerbie. Along with the worker's houses and blacksmith was a small hotel with the oddest name the Jolly Cripple, built in 1873. A new hotel, the Nottingham Castle, was built in 1877, and when this hotel applied for a license, the Jolly Cripple's license also came up for renewal. The licensing authority declared that two hotels were not required and awarded the license to the Nottingham Castle, so the Jolly Cripple had to close.

Business boomed as the hotel was an important coach stop on the way to the newly discovered Te Aroha goldfields, but while the hotel prospered Morrin did not, and after substantial financial loses in the 1880s depression, he left the country in the 1890s.

Fire swept through the Nottingham Castle around 5am on 20 June 1913. Immediately a new bar was set up and did great business as locals come to view the smouldering ruins. Given that the temperance movement's influence was at its height, it was surprising that the new hotel was not only so large, but also so finely constructed.

Today the hotel retains most of the original 1914 exterior, including the elegant belvedere and verandas along with green-glazed tiling and a very sturdy main wooden door. Along Studholme Street several of the original etched glass windows proudly proclaim, 'Farmers Club Room' and 'Commercial Room'.

While substantially altered inside, particularly the bar area, the reception and upstairs accommodation is more original. Upstairs is enormous, with all the rooms opening out to the veranda; a perfect perch for watching the Morrinsville world go by. The foyer is lined with excellent historical photos, including one of the current hotel nearing completion.

Matching the upstairs, the huge main bar has a focus on sport and horse racing, with numerous televisions showing a wide variety of sports events. Next door is an onsite TAB and, while not flash, it is friendly and has its appeal.

THE GRAND TAVERN

81 Whitaker St, Te Aroha
Ph: 07 884 7576
Built: 1902
Heritage category 1
Food: Good hearty pub food from a kitchen used to satisfying large appetites.

In the late nineteenth century Te Aroha developed a reputation as a spa town based on the unique natural hot soda water from springs at the base of the mountain. Set around the domain are several Edwardian bathhouses of which the main facility, the 1898 Cadman Bath House, is now the local museum. Built in 1902, the Grand was one of several hotels catering for the growing number of tourists. It competed with the Hot Springs Hotel, the largest wooden hotel in New Zealand, directly across Whitaker Street from the Grand. Today the Grand Tavern still exudes Victorian charm and blends in perfectly with the old buildings of the Domain, while its rival hotel was unfortunately demolished in 1970.

The exterior of the wooden two-storey hotel is largely original, with a fine old veranda along the entire front of the hotel; and at street level the old windows with their half round tops are particularly attractive. While few original features remain inside, the current owners have endeavoured to preserve the traditional flavour and have created a charming small dining room that is a favourite with locals, and a friendly bar that is welcoming to visitors.

HARBOUR VIEW HOTEL

14 Bow Street, Raglan
Ph: 07 825 8010
Web: www.harbourviewhotel.co.nz
Built: 1902
Heritage category 2

Food: Eating at the Harbour View is part of the Raglan experience. The menu is varied, ranging from bars snacks and lighter meals through to more substantial fare. The seafood chowder is appropriately the specialty of the house.

Accommodation: Clean, tidy rooms with shared facilities, with access to the upstairs veranda.

Looming like an ocean liner over the main street of Raglan, the Harbour View Hotel is impossible to miss and is everything a Victorian pub should be. Deep ornate verandas run the length of the street frontage, the original sash windows are still in place, the floors are of old polished wood and the fine wooden staircase leads to the guest rooms. The raised ground floor veranda is particularly popular as the perfect spot to have a beer, a glass of wine or a coffee and watch the world go by.

Maybe the hotel reflects its first owner, the formidable Rachel McGregor, who arrived in New Zealand in 1835 at the age of five speaking only Gaelic, but quickly learnt both English and Maori. With her husband George, she built the hotel in 1866 and lived in Raglan until she died in 1926, at the age of 99. In the early hours of 14 December 1901,

the Harbour View was burned to the ground, but was quickly rebuilt in exactly the same style by the end of 1902.

Today the Harbour View is the heart of the busy coastal town of Raglan. The huge shaded garden bar, once famous as a live music venue hosting both local and international musicians, still attracts the summer crowds. The dining room runs across the front of the building, overlooking the main street. With the polished wood fixtures giving the room a warm ambience, this is a popular place for a casual lunch or a dinner out. You will need to be quick to bag a spot on the elevated veranda overlooking the main street.

WHAT'S IN A NAME?

Most New Zealand hotels are named after their locations without too much imagination, but several generic names occur throughout the country. The most common is the Railway, but there is also a good number of Royal, Commercial, Empire, Club, Masonic, Criterion, and Crown hotels. Masonic is a more common North Island hotel name than in the south. Names changed regularly and frequently moved from pub to pub with the license, often making the history of the pub difficult to follow. The traditional English pub names, such as Pig and Whistle and Cock and Bull, were unusual in early New Zealand hotels. The oddest name of all must go to a hotel built in Morrinsville in 1873: cheerfully named the Jolly Cripple.

COMMERCIAL HOTEL

97 Alexandra Street, Te Awamutu
Ph: 07 871 6100
Built: 1938
Food: Bistro meals, a blend of contemporary and traditional.

Since 1887, the Commercial Hotel has been a feature of Te Awamutu's main street. Originally a two-storey wooden hotel, the Commercial burnt down in 1937, was rebuilt in the fashionable art moderne style and opened the following year. The façade today is largely original, and the recent renovations have further enhanced the 1930s influences, resulting in a style that its comfortable yet modern. -

Open, airy and relaxed, the Commercial now has two large dining areas and bars. The more casual Peach and Porker bistro opens on the main street, while the Long Acre is more formal. Both names reflect local history, with the Long Acre referring to the practice of grazing cattle on the grass strip along roadsides. The Peach and Porker bar has more of a story behind it. Te Awamutu in the late nineteenth century was well known for its peach orchards, and one of the historical photos in the hotel shows a horse-drawn cart outside the Commercial loaded with boxes of peaches. It was also common for pigs to be fed on the windfall peaches under the trees. Another photo from the same period shows a young man, Edward Trumpton, walking his pet pig Nero in front of the hotel. Local folklore has it that Nero was last seen near the rear of the Commercial Hotel, never to reappear.

ALEXANDRA HOTEL

815 Franklin Street, Pirongia
Ph: 07 871 9838
Built: 1932
Food: Contemporary meets pub food in an excellent range of meals and snacks.
Accommodation: Stylish, clean rooms; three double and
one with three beds, with shared facilities.

Pirongia, originally known as Alexandra, was a key frontier town established at the end of the Land Wars in 1864 (an old redoubt still exists), and in the 1870s was the terminal port for paddle steamers on the Waipa River. However, the town declined when the new railway line south bypassed the town in favour of Te Awamutu and in 1896, to avoid confusion with Alexandra in Central Otago, the town was renamed Pirongia.

Built in 1864, the Alexandra retains the name of the old town and is the oldest hotel in the Waikato. In 1870, the license was transferred to the Doncaster Hotel, which was renamed the Alexandra (the former Alexandra hotel burnt down in 1875). In June 1932 fire claimed this hotel, but it was quickly rebuilt and opened in December of the same year. Finally closed down in 1999, the Alexandra remained empty for 15 years.

Transformed by Julie and Tony Penwarden, the hotel was completely renovated and refurbished, reopening again in 2015. Dating from 1930, the older section of the hotel has been completely restored and a new addition, the Five Stags, was built. Five Stags is a stylish combination of café, bar and restaurant; contemporary yet very rustic, historic hunting and local photos line the walls, and over the bar are five enormous stag heads of Sika, Whitetail, Red, Fallow and Rusa deer.

Now a firm favourite for both locals and visitors, the Alexandra is not just a place to call in while passing, it's well worth making the journey.

NATIONAL HOTEL/
ALPHA STREET KITCHEN AND BAR

47 Alpha Street, Cambridge
Ph: 07 827 5596
Built: 1912
Heritage category 2
Food: Alpha Street Kitchen and Bar offers stylish, contemporary food for lunch and dinner, plus small plates and an excellent offering of wines and beers.

Built in 1866, the first hotel on this site was the Alpha, which later changed to the National Hotel, affectionately known to the locals as the Nash. By 1906 a local police report condemned the hotel, which only had one bathroom to serve 27 bedrooms, although it did have seven sitting rooms. Basic repairs enabled the hotel to retain its

license until, in 1912 – and just after the transfer of the license to a new owner – the hotel was engulfed by fire. Rebuilt in brick by local builder Fred Potts, the new hotel that opened in 1912 was a good deal more modern in both style and comfort, with plenty of bathrooms for its 24 rooms. Eclectic in style, the building combined Classical, Spanish Mission, Scottish and Italian architectural elements, resulting in a handsome building that compliments the historic Cambridge Town Hall (1909) and the fine art deco Clock Tower (1934).

For the next 90 years the National was a popular local hotel, before closing and falling into disrepair. Avoiding the fate of many old New Zealand hotels, the National has been repurposed and today is mostly offices. However, an echo of the hospitality of the old hotel still lingers in the Alpha Street Kitchen and Bar, a contemporary restaurant the occupies the corner of the building, including a wide terrace that runs along the front of the old hotel overlooking Victoria Square.

OKOROIRE HOTEL

18 Somerville Road, Okoroire
Ph: 07 883 4876
Web: www.okohotel.co.nz
Built: 1884
Heritage category 2
Food: Contemporary menu with a focus on seasonal and local produce.
Accommodation: Twenty-one rooms, all en suite; thirteen in the
historic hotel and the remainder in an annex behind the hotel.

Long known to Maori for their healing properties, the Okoroire hot springs also began attracting Europeans. The road from Tirau to Rotorua was completed in 1883 and the Okoroire hotel opened in 1884, catering for tourists and travellers who visited the springs on the way to Rotorua and Taupo. Comprising of 76 acres, the first licensee, Mrs Isaacs, also oversaw the construction of four baths and is said to be responsible for the development of the hotel grounds including many of the fine old trees that remain, especially the avenue of plane trees.

Today the historic Okoroire Hotel is one of New Zealand's most iconic hotels and visitors are not only attracted by the hot springs, but also to this handsome building. The hotel still retains the original grounds, now with the addition of a nine hole golf course and a pleasant bush walk down to the pools.

Although the hotel has been altered over time, both the exterior and interior are largely original. The long accommodation wing of the hotel, with its original sash windows and long veranda running the full length of the single-storey building, is typically Victorian. The central part of the hotel also retains its Victorian charm, though the entrance was altered in the 1920s. Inside the hotel is a delight; renovated where possible and tastefully restored elsewhere, all reflecting an era of grace and elegance. The restaurant can cater for up to 100 people, but is in two sections so never feels overcrowded, and includes a large outdoor area. The small lounge at the front of the hotel, complete with open fire, reflects Edwardian comfort. On the opposite site from the accommodation wing is the main bar, which is typical of many Kiwi pubs, and off that a sunny deck is perfect for a quiet drink on a hot summer day. It is not surprising that the Okoroire appeals as much to local farmers as it does to visitors from New Zealand and beyond.

PUTARURU HOTEL

79 Princes St, Putaruru
Ph: 07 8833911
Web: www.putaruruhotel.co.nz
Built: 1953
Food: Specialising in ribs and steak and including salads, burgers and pizza.
Accommodation: 21 rooms upstairs, a bit dated but all en suite.

Just a short distance off SH1 and in need of restoration, the Putaruru Hotel is probably the finest original mid-century hotel in New Zealand.

The exterior hasn't been altered since the day it opened in 1953. There is an echo of art deco in the wide curved frontage that makes up the central part of the hotel. The striking original red tiled roof is more Mediterranean than south Waikato. The covered

90

entranceway evokes grand occasions when the arriving guest would drive up to the front door – all that is missing is the red carpet (and a good paint job). The foyer is pure 1950s, from the wooden panelling in the reception to a grand staircase, flanked by vertical frosted lights, which sweeps up to the bedrooms. The dedicated telephone booth still retains the glass doors, etched with the image of a telephone in case you are not sure where to go. Next door is the 'writing room' where guests would pen a few words on postcards about their grand time in Putaruru, and travelling salesmen wrote up their daily orders. Beyond the foyer are grand receptions rooms and the 'house bar', where guests could drink to the wee small hours. All now looks abandoned and in need of attention.

A sign reading 'Cook' marks the entrance to the pleasant, if somewhat scruffy, main bar. It is not that much different from 100 other public bars. However, it is a work in progress for the current owners, who have a long-term plan to restore rather than renovate this fine hotel.

ROTORUA

THE PRINCE'S GATE BOUTIQUE HOTEL

1057 Arawa Street, Rotorua
Ph: 07 348 1179
Web: www.princesgate.co.nz
Built: 1897
Heritage category 2
Accommodation: 34 boutique hotel rooms in the main building and 17 apartments in an adjoining building.
Food: The hotel offers an extensive menu for breakfast, lunch and dinner, combining traditional favourites with contemporary tastes.

Appearances can be deceiving. This fine Victorian hotel appears to be part of the very fabric of Rotorua, but in fact the Prince's Gate began life elsewhere. Originally the hotel was built in Waihi as the New Central Hotel, but after the Ohinemuri Electorate went dry in 1908, the hotel was closed the following year. As was common at the time, wooden buildings were often moved and reused, and in 1917 the New Central was dismantled and railed in pieces to Rotorua, where it was rebuilt in 1921. The hotel was renamed the Prince's Gate, reflecting its position directly opposite the elaborate wooden arch that commemorates the visit to Rotorua by the Duke and Duchess of York in 1901. The original hotel at Waihi had an incredible 75 rooms, many of which

would have been tiny single rooms, but today the hotel today has just 34 somewhat more spacious rooms.

Exuding a wonderful old-world charm, the hotel features huge leadlight windows, wooden panelling, elegant chandeliers, a grand staircase and period furniture. The wraparound Victorian verandas upstairs are for guests only and are the perfect place to watch the busy goings on in the street below and in the Government Gardens opposite. The Gate Bar and the Club dining room successfully combine yesteryear elegance with modern style and are perfectly complimented by the north facing garden bar. High tea on the ground floor terrace at street level is particularly popular.

COROMANDEL & BAY OF PLENTY

COROMANDEL

ROYAL OAK HOTEL, TAPU

SH 25, Tapu, 20km north of Thames
Ph: 07 8684 806
Built: 1933
Food: Huge menu of pub favourites from bar snacks to main meals at excellent prices. As well as the meal and bar snacks there are also separate menus for burgers, lunch, children's and gluten-free food. Impossible not to find something to your taste, the pub is popular with families and especially children.

The first Royal Oak hotel was a fine two-storied structure built in the mid-1880s to service the coach trade up to Coromandel to the north and over the rugged ranges to Coroglen in the east. Classically Victorian in style with verandas overlooking the road, the hotel burnt down in 1933 with the death of a local miner who was staying in the hotel. Rebuilt, this time as a low single-story building, the pub today is a firm favourite with locals, visitors and especially fishers and more often than not there is a vehicle with a boat in tow parked outside.

While the interior is bright, modern and clean, the pub is particularly famous for its beer garden – well sheltered from the westerly winds. From the bar and restaurant the view is over a typically kiwi camping ground across the road and beyond to the Firth of Thames. A section of the wall features numerous historical photos of both the pub and the coast, including pictures of the famous Auckland trams that ended up as small holiday homes.

700 Pollen Street, Thames
Ph: 07 868 6008
Web: www.thejunction.net.nz
Built: 1869
Heritage category 2
Food: Hearty pub meals and snacks, which are better than average,
matched by a good range of beers, wines and cocktails. Open
for lunch and dinner, and for breakfast on the weekend.
Accommodation: 17 renovated rooms designed to suit every
budget, ranging from en suite through to dormitory beds.

When gold was discovered in Thames in August 1867, gold miners from all over the globe set sail for New Zealand. Within a short period the local population reached 11,000 people, as big as Auckland at the time. Along with the miners came the merchants, including hoteliers, and by 1872 the town boasted two breweries and 112 hotels, though many of these were mere wooden facades with the rest of the building made of canvas. Today just three pubs remain, and the Junction is one of these.

Thames at the time was two distinct settlements – Shortland to the south and Grahamstown to the north – and the junction between the two was the Karaka Stream. When a hotel was built at the junction in 1869 the choice of name was obvious.

Recently restored, the Junction today would be easily recognised by a time traveller from the gold rush days. The main bar on the corner of Pollen and Pahau Street, with its extensive use of wood, polished floors and historic photos and sketches, is both stylish and functional, and the atmosphere is warm and welcoming. A sports bar is behind the hotel, with the main entrance off Pahau Street. On the corner, café seating catches the afternoon sun, the ideal spot to settle in for a cool drink after a busy day.

GOLD RUSH DAYS

During the gold rushes of the nineteenth century it was not unusual in New Zealand for whole towns, and especially hotels, to literally spring up overnight. On the West Coast, Ross boasted 21 hotels, Hokitika 103 (84 in Revell Street alone), and Greymouth 57. Thames on the Coromandel had 113 hotels in its heyday, and Naseby in Central Otago had 22 hotels – 10% of the population were publicans. Many were very basic structures, some merely with a wooden façade and a canvas back. Some hotels were tiny, and in the original Stanley Hotel at McRaes Flat there was more space behind the bar than in front.

Prospectors would often arrive in town, cash up their gold at a hotel or bank and hand the money over to the publican, only leaving when their money ran out after blowing the lot on lodging, food and drink (and sometimes women). Arthur's Point Hotel near Queenstown was both an hotel and a bank.

COROMANDEL HOTEL

611 Kapanga Road, Coromandel
Ph: 07 866 8760
Web: www.coromandelhotel.co.nz
Built: Prior to 1862
Food: A large, bright restaurant offering a good range of food
and wines, with fresh local seafood a specialty.
Accommodation: The Coromandel has eight hotel rooms, that
are very smart and clean, with shared facilities. Behind the hotel
are simple backpacker units and a campervan park.

While gold was discovered in the Coromandel area in 1852, it wasn't until the 1860s that the town boomed in the heyday of the gold rushes. In 1862, to take advantage of the business opportunities in the flourishing gold town, the two-storey Kikowhakarere Hotel was moved into town and renamed the Coromandel Hotel. In the early 1930s the hotel suffered a major fire that destroyed the top floor. Never rebuilt, the hotel today is now just one storey.

Affectionately known as the 'top pub', the Coromandel retains all the atmosphere of a good country pub. The large main bar is spacious, with large folding windows opening out to the street; just the spot to have a quiet beer and watch the world go by. Photos of local sports teams, fishing trophies and memorabilia line the walls, while outside is a large beer garden, overhung with large shady trees and perfect on a hot summer afternoon. If you are looking for a bit of genuine Kiwi hospitality away from the 'flash' of Coromandel's trendy main street, then look no further than the Coromandel Hotel.

WHITIANGA HOTEL

1 Blacksmith Lane, Whitianga
Ph: 07 866 5818
Built: Around 1925
Food: The Salt Restaurant and Bar overlooking the marina must be one of Whitianga's smartest places to dine. The menu is sophisticated and modern, the service and wine list excellent, and the location alongside the water and under the huge Phoenix palms is hard to beat. Whitianga Hotel has an excellent variety of good pub food at equally good prices.

The Whitianga Hotel has plenty of personality, and the two halves of the hotel are very different. The side of the hotel housing Salt Restaurant and Bar and overlooking the marina has all the feel of a smart, beach resort restaurant. Relaxed, modern and stylish, this is the place to spend the evening eating and drinking on a balmy summer's evening, though of course all this comes at a price.

Next door, the Whitianga Hotel pub couldn't be more different. Spacious, open and with a huge garden bar complete with a stage, the atmosphere here is informal and relaxed. Here the focus is on entertainment, with year-round live music, including the famous New Year's Eve bash.

The hotel has a lively history as well. The original hotel was built in 1886, by Thomas Carina, when the township moved from Ferry Landing to the other side of the river. Burnt down around 1925, the hotel was rebuilt, only to be hit again by fire in March 1956. In recent years Whitianga town has flourished and, like the town, the Whitianga Hotel is destined to flourish for some time to come.

Tairua Whitianga Road/SH25, Coroglen
Ph: 07 866 3809
Web: coroglentavern.co.nz
Built: 1946
Food: Good country food with a contemporary twist.

Originally the hotel was built down by the river, in 1879, when Coroglen was known by the unglamorous name of Gumtown, reflecting the town's reliance on kauri gum rather than gold or timber. In its heyday around 1900, the hotel boasted 25 bedrooms; but like so many Coromandel towns, the population declined, and the gum diggers were long gone when the town changed its name to Coroglen in 1922, after a famous racehorse. Burnt down and moved several times, the current pub dates from 1946.

Today the Coroglen Tavern is justifiably one of New Zealand's iconic pubs. Skillfully combining the rustic with the modern, the pub is famous as a summer music venue, attracting crowds of around 2,000 to gigs featuring the best of New Zealand's musicians.

However, it is just a great place to kick back and relax in the very best New Zealand style. Timber from the old sales yard, memorabilia, the corrugated iron façade, historic photos, the bar made from great slab of macrocarpa and the old wool presses link the pub to its long past. This is just the place to grab a good coffee, a cold beer or good country food with a contemporary twist. Kick back, settle down and watch the world go by from the veranda that runs along the entire front of the building.

THE STERLING TAVERN

112 Seddon St, Waihi
Ph: 07 863 6395
Built: 1922
Food: The menu is extensive and surprisingly varied. In addition
to the large menu there are also blackboard specials.

The Sterling Tavern now sits at the quieter end of Waihi's busy main street and, while not so good for business, the diversion of the traffic on the busy roads to Whangamata and Tauranga makes for a very pleasant experience for customers. Built in 1897, the Sterling was the terminus for the busy coach route from Waihi through the Karangahake gorge to Paeroa. Located directly opposite the main gates of the prosperous Martha Mine, the Sterling was locally known as the 'miners pub'. Stories tell of how the mine tunnellers, who had a depot nearby, dug a tunnel to the back of the Stirling Hotel so they could sneak across to the pub for a quick drink at lunch time. At the time it was common for the wives of miners to wait at the mine gates to collect their husband's pay, and thereby prevent the men from spending all their earnings in the local pubs. It is believed that the miners also used the secret tunnel to by-pass the women and get to the Sterling.

On 11 March 1918, fire destroyed three buildings, including the pub, as well as damaging several other buildings.

Tucked away on the wall is a framed collection of pub treasures. The main photo shows the old wooden hotel, along with a lengthy newspaper account of the destructive fire, and the first license issued to the pub on 2 June 1897, at the cost of 25 pounds. Also in the frame are two beer labels for Red Seal Pale Ale and Red Seal Stout, from the time the pub brewed its own beer.

Comfortable and friendly, the main bar and dining room occupies the entire corner on Seddon and Mueller streets, and beyond that is a pool room and a small garden bar. It is the only pub in Waihi where you can sit and have a cool ale under umbrellas on the street, perfect on a hot summer's day. Directly opposite the imposing Cornish pumphouse, the Sterling is very easy to find and there's always plenty of parking for those walking up to view the spectacular Martha opencast mine.

WAIKINO HOTEL

8541 SH 2, Waikino
Ph: 07 863 8381
Web: www.waikinohotel.nz
Built: In Mackeytown in 1898 and relocated to Waikino in 1926.
Food: Bistro style menu offering both homestyle family
favourites and dishes for the more adventurous.

The first Waikino Hotel was built by Mr Montgomery in 1896, at the heart of the bustling Waikino township. The busy hotel serviced the local gold mines and the enormous 200 stamper Victoria Battery just across the Ohinemuri River, but it was engulfed by a raging inferno in 1906, along with several nearby stores. The hotel was gone, but the miners weren't, so the Waitekauri Hotel was dragged by bullock team to Waikino to replace it.

A few years later the region voted 'dry'. Unable to sell liquor, hotels became far less profitable and the second Waikino Hotel was demolished, its kauri timber sold to build cottages in Hamilton.

Six years passed before prohibition was lifted, and the Mackaytown Hotel was moved to Waikino from the other side of the rocky Karangahake Gorge. The Herculean effort was achieved in just one day by bullock teams, hauling the pub in two pieces over the hill (the gorge road didn't exist at the time). Publicans came and went, and the ghost stories multiplied. The hotel now hosts two resident ghosts, though exactly who these echoes from the past are is unclear. Local lore says the gent is Harold, an old miner who died in the first hotel, while the woman could be Alice Hamilton, a hotel cook who was murdered after being hit by a car not far down the road.

In 1981 torrential flooding hit Waikino, destroying everything but the hotel (then the Waikino Tavern) and the Victoria Hall. While businesses and homes were washed downriver, some tenacious locals kept drinking, moving the grog upstairs when the floodwaters rose too high.

By 2017 flood damage, neglect and constant shaking from trucks thundering past had left the Waikino Hotel worse for wear. Determined to save the hotel and restore it to the community hub it once was, the family owner-operators undertook a complete six-month renovation to replace crumbling foundations and recreate some of the hotels historic features. Inside has been wonderfully restored, with local mining memorabilia and historic photos lining the walls, while the exterior has been painstakingly stripped, repaired and painted in historic colours. The warm wood interior and impressive bar are complemented by the friendly local atmosphere, the hearty food served in the beautiful dining room and the sunny sheltered courtyard.

THE TEMPERANCE MOVEMENT

During the second half of the nineteenth century and the early years of the twentieth century, the movement for the restriction of alcohol grew in strength. The movement was partly religion-based, but it was also an early expression of the growing influence of women on politics, and is often closely linked with the rise of feminism. It was women who bore the brunt of excessive drinking, through both increased domestic violence and through the poverty caused by alcohol gobbling up a significant share of the household income. Working men were often paid daily or weekly in cash, and it was not uncommon for wives to gather outside the work place to ensure their husbands didn't disappear off to the pub.

With the combination of both the temperance movements and women's votes, many areas voted to go 'dry', beginning with Clutha in 1894, and in 1911 legislation was passed to allow a national poll on prohibition. The closest New Zealand came to prohibition was during the election of 1919, with initial results showing a slight majority in favour of a liquor ban, though this was later overturned by postal votes from soldiers overseas. Later that year a further poll was held, with the prohibitionists missing out by only 3,300 votes. While the movement remained strong in the 1920s and 30s, the prohibitionists never again came close to banning the sale of alcohol.

BAY OF PLENTY

THE TALISMAN HOTEL

7-9 Main Road/SH2, Katikati
Ph: 07 549 3218
Web: www.talismanhotel.co.nz
Built: Around 1930
Food: An excellent menu of contemporary dishes
that are available for lunch and dinner.
Accommodation: Five rooms all en suite.

The settlement of Katikati by immigrants from Ulster was determined by the access from Tauranga up the Uretara River. The first hotel – called the Uretara Hotel and established around 1876 by a Mrs Bell – was originally down by the river below the current pub. In 1880 the pub was run by Bernard McDonnell, who stood 6'2" tall, weighed over 20 stone and was a Catholic, unusual in this staunchly Protestant town. In 1888 McDonnell's young son was swept away in the river and drowned. Broken-hearted, he sold the pub to Alfred Shepard. With substantial financial interests in the Talisman mine in the Karangahake Gorge, Shepherd not only renamed the hotel, but moved the pub away from the river to its present site. Destroyed by fire in March 1929, the pub standing today was built in 1930.

The Talisman is a popular one-stop eating and drinking spot in Katikati for both locals and travellers. The Landings Restaurant and Garden Bar is smart and comfortable, and it opens out to a lovely, shady garden behind the hotel. An open fire adds to the cosy atmosphere on cooler winter days. The Talisman also has a very extensive selection of wines by the glass and bottle. The main bar features old photos of Katikati, a big screen television and a warm atmosphere for a relaxing ale.

WHAKATANE HOTEL

79 The Strand, Whakatane
Ph: 07 307 1670
Built: 1939
Food: The Craic Irish Pub serves a wide range of bar snacks, pizzas and Irish themed meals at very reasonable prices. The menu varies between summer and winter, and the hotel has the only wood-fired pizza oven in town.
Accommodation: 30 clean and tidy upstairs rooms with a range of options, from en suite to single through to backpackers. The Boiler Room is a popular late night bar, so the rooms can be noisy at night.

The large and imposing Whakatane Hotel was built in 1939 in a late burst of art deco style, and today the building is tastefully painted in green and cream. The interior still retains some original features, including a fine staircase overlooked by art deco leadlight windows.

Essentially this is a hotel of two parts, and they couldn't be more different. On the corner is The Craic, an Irish themed bar and restaurant complete with dark wood, cosy seating and a homely atmosphere, with an outdoor seating area on the street. A good variety of meals are available and the bar has excellent range of beers on tap, including Guinness, Kilkenny and Oranjeboom from South Africa. The Boiler Room next door is Whakatane's leading nightclub and definitely not the place for a quiet drink. Decorated in an industrial chic style with an actual boiler that pumps out steam, this bar attracts a younger crowd with big name groups, and on a good night is packed out after 11pm. The large garden bar off The Boiler Room allows the party people a chance for a bit of fresh air.

ROYAL HOTEL

Cnr King and Church Street, Opotiki
Ph: 07 315 8840, 027 555 0935
Built: 1879
Food: The Royal restaurant is simply decorated but smart with a menu
that covers all the bases and has a good reputation with locals.
Accommodation: Good clean bright backpackers with shared facilities.

Constructed entirely of native timber the Royal Hotel in the main street of Opotiki was built in 1879. After being extensively damage by both flood and fire in the early twentieth century, the hotel underwent considerable reconstruction to become an impressive hotel with 50 rooms. Despite many alterations over the years the Royal today still features its original exterior and inside retains the original kauri staircase, a mixture of rimu and kauri floors and architectural details from a bygone era.

The hotel was for some time the home of Fannie Rose Howie who rose to fame in the early twentieth century for her Maori lullaby Hine-e-hine. Of Ngati Porou descent Fannie, who was also known as Pane Poata and Te Rangi Pai, was born in Tokomaru Bay on January 11th 1868. After studying music in New Zealand and Australia, she toured Britain to much acclaim in early years of the twentieth century. Returning to New Zealand in 1905, Fannie composed her most famous song Hine-e-hine in 1907. With her health failing Fannie was living at the Royal where she died on the 20th of May 1916 in a room directly above the bar. A gentle presence believed to be the spirit of Fannie is still felt in the hotel.

Time has not been kind to either Opotiki or the Royal. The upstairs accommodation is now a backpackers with shared facilities which are clean and tidy and for some time the bar and restaurant were closed. Now reopened and simply known as The Royal, the restaurant is spacious, simply decorated with a superb, polished floor and friendly atmosphere.

MASONIC HOTEL

121 Church Street, Opotiki
Ph: 07 315 6115
Built: 1916/1918
Heritage Category 2
Food: The restaurant unusually has two menus, one offering
traditional pub meals and the other Indian dishes.
Accommodation: Eleven simple clean rooms with shared facilities.

Opotiki's sturdy Masonic Hotel, with its grand Edwardian façade, is built to last. The first two hotels were destroyed by fire; the first dating from around 1860 and the second built in 1895. Demolished and rebuilt in 1916 with stucco over a double and a triple brick heart, it was thought that this building was unlikely to go up in flames as did the two predecessors – but the hotel was again hit by fire in 1918. Badly damaged, the hotel was extensively modified when rebuilt. The Masonic today has a main bar with original arched windows, and a popular Irish bar and restaurant with a small outdoor courtyard.

The Irish bar retains many of the hotel's original features, including walls attractively stripped back to the time-aged brickwork, and even the old coal range from the time when that part of the hotel was the kitchen. Old photographs of both the hotel and Opotiki line the walls, including several of the destructive flood of 1964, showing the whole of central Opotiki deep under water. The original wood panelling in the hotel foyer still exists, as does the fine wooden staircase leading to the first floor. For guests there is a spacious lounge with a small balcony that gives a great vantage point over Opotiki's main street.

Across the road is the historical St Stephen's Church, scene of the murder of Reverend Völkner during the Hauhau uprisings, and a few doors down is the restored De Luxe Theatre, home to the Silent Movie Film Festival held each year in September.

WAIHAU BAY LODGE

51 Orete Point Road, Waihau Bay
Ph: 07 325 3805
Web: www.thewaihaubaylodge.co.nz
Built: 1904
Food: Good pub meals including breakfast, naturally strong in fresh seafood.
Accommodation: Six budget rooms with shared facilities, opening out on to a veranda with incredible views across the bay and three self contained units.

Retaining its original Edwardian exterior, the Waihau Bay has some of the most incredible views of any hotel in New Zealand. Sheltered by a low headland, the pub faces the Pacific Ocean, out over Waihau Bay and across to rugged Cape Runaway in the distance. Whales were hunted in the rich waters of this coast right up until the 1920s, and today the area boasts some of New Zealand's best deep sea fishing. From the comfort of the bar, patrons can watch the comings and goings on the boat ramp and weigh station right opposite the hotel, and it is not unusual to see marlin being hauled ashore. For more modest recreational fisher folk the area has excellent fishing in general, including yellow-finned tuna in the season, and legendary snapper. The National Big Game Fishing week is held over 10 days at the end of February, and over 100 boats are launched daily from Waihau Bay boat ramp.

Today the hotel has a large dining room with folding doors opening out onto a broad terrace, and next door the bar has wide doors and windows which give an uninterrupted view of the activity across the road and out over the bay.

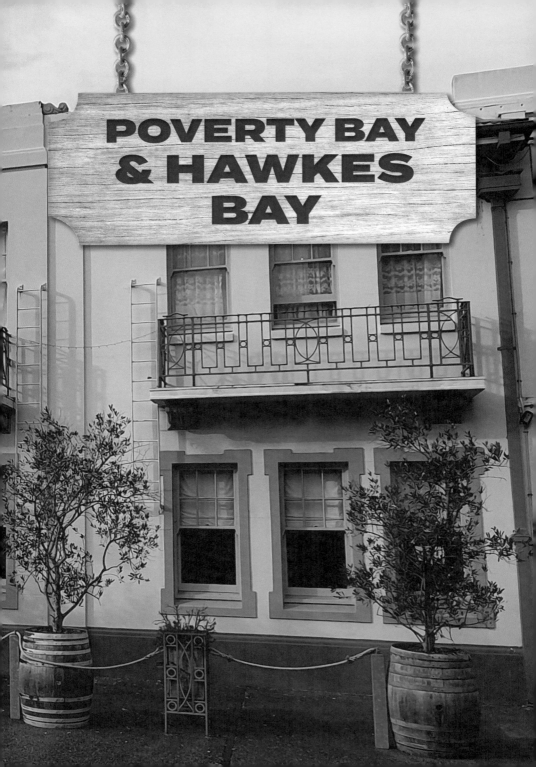

POVERTY BAY

TOLAGA BAY INN

Corner Cook and Solander Streets/SH 35, Tolaga Bay
Ph: 06 862 6856
Web: www.tolagabayinn.co.nz
Built: 1933
Food: Uawa Café occupies the old corner lounge bar and offers light meals, snacks, cakes and coffee, all made on the premises, and it is a popular stopping point on Highway 35.
Accommodation: Five backpacker rooms with shared facilities, and upstairs lounge with a small balcony overlooking the highway.

The imposing Tolaga Bay Inn is easy to spot. With its distinct high-pitched tile roof and Tudor style, the hotel dwarfs and dazzles its more simple neighbours in the sleepy beach settlement of Tolaga Bay. Designed by renowned architect Shalto Smith, the current building was constructed during the summer of 1932-1933 and received its license in

1934. This replaced a much larger hotel near the river, dating back to 1889, which burnt down in suspicious circumstances some years before. Although the building has had a least two extensions, including an ungainly concrete block wing in the 70s, the Tolaga still retains most of it fine original features. The mock-Tudor design is overlaid with very attractive Arts and Crafts features, that include beautiful wood panelling and leadlight windows (now part of the cafe) and heraldic plaster crests (partially obscured by the fire escapes). A smaller bar just off the main entrance is known as the ANZAC room and has an impressive carved wooden fire place.

On the middle landing of the staircase is a painting entitled *Night and Morn*. The painting, similar in style to a leadlight window, consists of two painted panels, one of an owl and the other of a windmill, separated by the text 'Life is like a staircase, some are coming up and some are going down.' Above and below the words are the enigmatic letters GSTW and CSAN, whose meaning remains a mystery.

In addition to the Uawa Café, the Tolaga also acts as the local information centre. In the rough and ready public bar is a huge macrocarpa slab, creating what must be the widest bar surface of any hotel in the country. Time has not been kind to the Tolaga Inn and currently the local Trust, which owns the pub, has plans to restore this exceptional example of Arts and Craft design in New Zealand.

BUSHMERE ARMS

Main Road/SH 2, Waerenga-a-Hika, Gisborne
Ph: 06 862 5820
Web: www.bushmerearms.co.nz
Built: 1870s
Food: With an excellent al la carte menu that certainly could not be described as 'pub food', the Bushmere is the perfect spot for an elegant lunch or a night out.

The Bushmere Arms began life as the Waerenga-a-Hika Hotel, when Robert Colebrook was granted a license in 1873. However, it is uncertain if the current hotel building dates from this period as there is evidence of a fire, though whether this completely destroyed the hotel is unknown. A painting on the inn wall shows Waerenga-a-Hika as a thriving settlement in the late nineteenth century, with two hotels, a blacksmith, stores, and numerous houses. The township, which has largely disappeared, serviced the ferry that crossed the Waipoua River behind the hotel, and the road next to the Bushmere Arms still bears the name Ferry Road. A local story tells of a publican who drowned in the river and whose ghost apparently still haunts the area.

Bushmere Arms has been lovingly renovated from a near derelict state, and today is a beautiful small inn that is well worth the 14km journey from Gisborne. The restaurant and front bar are lined in natural wood panelling sourced from another demolished hotel, while the huge totara beams in the main dining area were washed down the river during Cyclone Bola. The pub was badly flooded in the 1948 flood, but the stop banks held during Cyclone Bola and the district escaped flooding that had plagued the area in earlier years. Wisteria twists along the old verandas and along the top of the bar is an impressive collection of over 300 ceramic whiskey jugs.

The cosy back bar is ideal for a quiet drink or a game of pool, and this in turn leads out to a spacious terrace and the wood-fired pizza oven.

A more recent addition is the large function/dining area, with the extensive use of wood and low windows tastefully echoing the older part of the hotel. Beyond this is a fabulous garden in a broad T shape and traditional style, with low hedging, rose gardens, pergolas and a covered gazebo. It is not surprising that the Bushmere Arms is a popular wedding venue.

The hotel is now a far cry from the old Waerenga-a-Hika Hotel that a Licensing Commission inspector in 1964 commented that 'I can state with reasonable certainty that only the most desperate fugitive would want to stay on the premises as a paying guest.'

HAWKES BAY

THE WESTSHORE BEACH INN

85 Meeanee Quay, Westshore, Napier
Ph: 06 835 9879
Web: www.westshorebeachinn.co.nz
Built: 1926
Food: The Westshore has two dining areas, one offering innovative Asian flavours with a strong Philippino flavour, while the other has a more traditional, pub style menu.
Accommodation: 15 studios of varying size, both upstairs in the hotel and in a more recently built substantial motel-like complex behind the hotel, with very reasonable rates.

Tucked away from the art deco of central Napier, the Westshore Inn is one of the few public buildings to survive the 1931 earthquake and is a real gem of an early twentieth century New Zealand hotel. The Westshore has a long and varied history, starting out in 1851 as the McKains Villers Accommodation and then changing names to the Ahuriri and the Ferry, until that hotel burnt down. The new hotel was built in 1926 and the exterior of the hotel has altered little over the years, though it has been substantially extended over time and is much bigger than it looks from the outside.

Exuding a relaxed atmosphere, the Westshore is Napier's only BrewPub, producing nine different beers under the Napier Brewing Co label. The brewing area sits alongside the Sports Bar and can be viewed through the huge glass windows. The main restaurant harks back to an earlier era, with old oak furniture from the 20s and 30s, while there are also several outdoor areas for a quiet drink in the sun or shade. A popular local pub, the Westshore Inn is well worth checking out on any visit to the Hawkes Bay.

UNION HOTEL

3 Waghorne Street, Ahuriri, Napier
Ph: 06 835 1274 (Union Hotel)
Ph: 06 834 0835 (Fourth Door Lounge Bar and Three Doors Up Restaurant)
Built: 1931

Established in 1861 as the Commercial Hotel, the name was changed to the Union Hotel in 1887. In March 1917 the hotel narrowly missed being completely destroyed in a major fire that badly damaged the front of the building. Escaping destruction by fire, the Union was destroyed in the Hawkes Bay earthquake of 1931 and was rebuilt that same year, this time in the highly fashionable Spanish Mission style and using reinforced concrete and brick.

Cleverly repurposed, the old Union Hotel is a pub of four parts. The original upstairs accommodation is now stylish apartments in popular Ahuriri. Downstairs are three separate components: The Union Hotel, Three Doors Up restaurant, and the Fourth Door Lounge.

Consisting of one large bar on the corner, entering the Union Hotel is like stepping back 30 years. Locals yarn over jugs of beer at high topped bar tables and, apart from the presence of women, it probably hasn't changed that much since the pub was built. Next door is the very stylish Three Doors Up restaurant, featuring a great contemporary menu and excellent wine list. However, best of all is the Fourth Door Lounge bar, an art deco themed piano and jazz bar tucked in behind the restaurant. Both the bar and the restaurant open onto a gorgeous sheltered courtyard.

Just down the street is the Crown Hotel, a Heritage category 2 building now housing the reception and function facilities for a much larger and modern complex. Still retaining the superb 1932 façade, take a peek inside the reception area for the stunning leadlight window, which features a crown.

ART DECO MASONIC HOTEL

2 Tennyson Street, Napier
Ph: 06 835 8689
Web: www.masonic.co.nz
Built: 1932
Food: Excellent gastro pub menu that will have a wide appeal.
Accommodation: Stylish rooms that feature the hotel's art deco heritage.
The rooms, along with the central location and the upstairs terrace
overlooking Marine Parade, make the Masonic hard to beat.

The history of the Masonic Hotel is both a history of the hotel industry and of Hawke's Bay rolled into one. Established in 1861, the first hotel, like many wooden New Zealand hotels, was burnt to the ground in 1896. Rebuilt in1897, this Masonic was a grand building with wide verandas facing the ocean across Marine Parade. This hotel was completely destroyed in the 1931 earthquake. The new Masonic built in 1932 was not only made of concrete, but also designed in the most fashionable and modern style of the day, art deco. The upstairs rooms are built around two open courtyards, and across the front of the building is a wide terrace that is just the perfect spot to watch the comings and goings along Marine Parade. The highlight is the stylish sunroom, overlooking the water and furnished with period cane chairs. The sunroom, along with the exterior and the foyers, still retains the original art deco features.

Until recently the Masonic made little of its art deco past, but all that has changed. With painstaking attention to detail, the Masonic has been completely transformed, and stepping into the Masonic today is stepping back into era of elegance sharped by sympathetic modern styling. In short it is plain fabulous and just makes you want to drink cocktails.

The main entrance to the hotel on Tennyson Street is covered by a small veranda, with the name 'Masonic' stylishly heralded in vintage leadlight glass, while the foyer itself is outfitted in dark wood panelling and period lighting. An outdoor terrace on Marine Parade is the perfect spot to take in the sea air. No visit to Napier is complete without a stop at the Masonic, one of New Zealand's most stylish hotels.

CLIVE HOTEL

Main Road, Clive
Ph: 06 8700 533
e: clivepub@xtra.co.nz
Built: 1931
Food: Contemporary menu, lighter meals and snacks, plus cakes and cabinet food.

Originally the Clive Hotel was built on the opposite bank of the Ngaruroro River, and was later moved to the present site. On Good Friday 1897, the hotel was the scene of great drama when, after a day of continuous rain, the river rose suddenly, forcing over 200 residents to take refuge in the two-storey hotel. Disaster struck when two of the three boats sent to rescue the stranded people overturned in the turbulent water, drowning the crew of both boats. Built of wood, the hotel was destroyed in the 1931 earthquake. Today's building dates from later that year.

Definitely a pub of two halves, the main bar is huge, traditional Kiwi bar; friendly, relaxed and just the place to watch sport and yarn with your mates. The other half is different. Accurately described as a lounge bar, this corner bar is stylishly designed and furnished with retro lounge suites. A mishmash of chairs and sofas from the 80s and 90s, nothing matches and most of the furniture is hideous, but together it all works, and the result is immensely appealing and attractive. Opening out onto a sunny deck, this is just the place for coffee and cake during the day or a cool drink as the sun goes down.

THE PUKETAPU

679 Puketapu Road, Western Hill, Hastings
Ph: 06 844 7206
Web: www.thepuketapu.co.nz
Built: 1910
Food: Something for everyone on this extensive menu. With
a focus on local produce, this is good country cooking with a
contemporary flair and at prices that are hard to beat.

Situated in a valley just a few kilometres north west of Taradale, in the late nineteenth century Puketapu was an important crossroads for travellers heading north to Wairoa and Gisborne and inland to Taupo and Taihape. In 1885 a substantial two-storey hotel was established to provide coaches with a change of horses and to feed and accommodate coach passengers, drivers delivering goods on bullock trains and drovers moving stock. Known as the Pheasants Nest and the Puketapu Hotel, this building was razed to the ground by fire in March 1909, a blaze which also destroyed the post office and store next door.

Extended in 1970, today the Puketapu is still at the centre of this local community and a popular destination for visitors from Hawkes Bay and further afield, especially those cycling the Puketapu loop of the Water Ride cycle trail.

The heart of the Puketapu is a large, friendly bar, which extends out into a spacious covered area and beyond that to a garden bar. With a comfortable country style, the adjoining dining area, decorated with historic photos and memorabilia, is the perfect spot to enjoy the extensive menu on offer. Live music on Sunday afternoons, excellent service and well-priced meals make the Puketapu an excellent detour on any trip to Hawkes Bay.

COACHING DAYS

While the usual focus of a pub is alcohol, early licensing requirements obliged the hotels to provide a certain standard of accommodation for both people and horses. Travel was long and arduous and many hotels owed their existence to their position as staging posts and ferry crossings. The Bushmere Arms once serviced the ferry crossing over the Waipoua River, and the Gladstone Hotel in the Wairarapa provided accommodation for travellers crossing the Ruamahanga. The Manutahi (Taranaki), Vulcan, Cardrona, Dansey Pass, Royal (Central Otago), Top House (Nelson), Wimbledon (Wairarapa), and even the Shepherds Arms in central Wellington all serviced coach routes. The hotels were often mini settlements and provided services such as a blacksmith, general store or post office, but today most of the outbuildings have disappeared.

TIKOKINO COUNTRY HOTEL/ SAWYERS ARMS

388 State Highway 50, Tikokino
Ph: 06 856 5446
Web: www.tikokinocountryhotel.co.nz
Built: 1864
Food: Small but innovative gastro pub menu in the restaurant, snacks and lighter meals in the café.
Accommodation: Seven stylish, comfortable rooms with shared facilities.

Originally planned as a railway settlement, Tikokino became primarily a timber town when the railway ended up being built well to the east. In its heyday, the township had 20 sawmills and that legacy is reflected in the name of the hotel: Sawyers Arms. Like many old hotels, the history of the Sawyers Arms is obscure, but the hotel was built in 1864 and is very typical style of a nineteenth century hotel so, despite rumours of a fire, it is unlikely to have been burnt down.

Now the hub of the tightknit community, the renamed Tikokino Country Hotel is as much a restaurant and café as a pub, and it is a popular destination for both locals and those on the less travelled SH50. Decorated in warm and friendly style, the main bar/café opens out to a lovely garden bar complete with a fenced children's playground. Weekly musical entertainment and regular events are held at the pub.

Whether you are after coffee and cake or a wine and beer, don't drive past this classic country pub.

THE BLACK DOG

835 Matamau Ormondville Road, Makotuku (near Norsewood)
Built: Around 1900
Ph: 027 857 4810
Food: A simple menu of burgers and chips, tasty and substantial.
Accommodation: Simple wooden cabins behind the pub, with shared facilities.

In August 1880 the railway line reached Makotuku, and the small township was the southern terminal of the Napier south line before the line was pushed through to Dannevirke in 1884. Obscured by time, not much is known about the old Makotuku Hotel, but the first license was granted on 9 June 1888 to Mr R Essex (on 30 June the nearby Beaconsfield Hotel obtained its first license). Apparently, the old hotel burned down sometime later, possibly in a large bush fire in 1898 that destroyed a number of buildings, including the church. The style of the existing hotel fits the time frame of around 1900. Once a thriving railway, timber mill and farming settlement, the population gradually drifted away, and with the town reduced to a handful of houses the Makotuku Hotel, like so many country hotels, closed down in 2004.

But time had not reckoned on the energetic Helen Upson, who purchased the hotel in 2012. With a passion for motorbikes, she set about turning the hotel into a destination for bike enthusiasts. Thoroughly renovated, today the Black Dog is a great place to relax, regardless of your enthusiasm for motorbikes. Reflecting Helen's personality (she also breeds and trains dogs), this is a friendly, lively pub, with the large bar opening out to a massive north facing deck and beyond that a wide swathe of grass, perfect for the kids to run around on.

Well worth the short detour off SH2.

PONGAROA HOTEL

Route 52, Pongaroa
Ph: 06 376 2864
Web: www.pongaroahotel.co.nz
Built: 1911
Food: Good range of pub meals including a range of
'Route 52' burgers – you won't go away hungry.

In the heart of the rugged hill country of southern Hawkes Bay, the Pongaroa Hotel is a cut above the usual rural pub. In the late nineteenth century, the town flourished with the anticipation that the new railway line would go through the district, but hopes were dashed when the line went further west through Pahiatua. Still, in 1911 a branch of the Bank of New Zealand opened in the town, housed in a substantial two-storey building. Closed in 1937, for more than ten years the bank was used as a private house, until in 1948 the old bank became the Pongaroa Hotel.

It may be isolated, but distance doesn't diminish the friendly welcome of a pub that is the de facto community centre. A montage of historic photos covers one wall in the main bar, and in the small dining room a finely etched window has survived from the BNZ days. Stroll outside through a very grand Edwardian door to an expanse of lawn, where the pub hosts the annual pig hunting competition along with speed shearing events. It's also a great space to let the kids run wild, while relaxing on the shady deck. While not really on the way to anywhere, if you are in the district the Pongaroa Hotel is a great place to take a break.

TARANAKI, WHANGANUI & MANAWATU

TARANAKI

AWAKINO HOTEL

4650 Main Rd (SH 3), Awakino
Ph: 06 752 9815
Built: 1904
Food: Good pub meals, burgers, lighter snacks and, of course, whitebait fritters – caught in the Awakino and said to be the best in the district.
Accommodation: Nine rooms, en suite and shared facilities.

The Awakino Hotel began life as a boarding house alongside the Awakino River, providing accommodation for travellers on the long slog between New Plymouth and Hamilton. When the area went 'wet' in the mid-1950s, there was a furious debate as to where a hotel would be sited: Awakino, or just down the coast at Mokau. The argument was abruptly ended in 1957 when the owner of the boarding house at Awakino declared that it was now the Awakino Hotel and he was the publican.

The oldest part of the building dates from around 1904, and over the years extensions were added onto the original boarding house, at different times and in various styles, resulting in a large, rambling collection of buildings. The large bar and dining area is as friendly and as Kiwi as it gets, and outside is a wide terrace and rustic garden bar centred on a large, spreading pohutukawa tree. The pub doubles as the club rooms for both the Tainui Pighunting Club and the Mokau Fishing Club, with massive pig heads taking pride of place above the bar, and a tall pole used for weighing pigs and large fish out in front. A wood fire keeps the place snug on cold winter nights.

WHANGAMOMONA HOTEL

6018 Ohura Road/ SH 43, Whangamomona
Ph: 06 762 5823
Web: www.whangamomonahotel.co.nz
Built: 1911
Heritage category 2
Food: A good range of pub meals, lighter snacks and good coffee.
Accommodation: Simple rooms, very clean and tidy, with shared facilities and access to the marvellous veranda over the main street. Also five new, self-contained units behind the hotel. This is a popular spot and it pays to book ahead, especially for the weekends.

Located in the heart of the Forgotten World Highway, the Whangamomona Hotel is legendary. The original hotel was built in 1902 to service both the railway between Taumaranui and Stratford and the growing farming community in the rugged Taranaki

back country. Burnt down in 1910, the replacement pub was rebuilt in 1911; though the original coal range from the old hotel, a solid Shacklock built in Dunedin, survived the fire and is still in the kitchen today. During the 1918-19 influenza epidemic, the hotel doubled as a hospital, and the old morgue is now used as a storage room. Whangamomona shot to fame when, in 1989, the district declared independence as a protest to redrawn local government boundaries that moved half the district from Taranaki into the Manawatu. The heart of the rebellion was the pub where the plot was hatched, and independence declared. Today the hotel still issues 'Whangamomona Republic Passports' and is the centre of the bi-annual (every odd numbered year) Republic Day celebrations in January, which attracts thousands to this tiny township with a population of just 15 people.

The Whangamomona Hotel today successfully achieves the ideal combination of rustic charm and modern facilities. The walls are lined with pictures of local sports teams, snapshots of local celebrities and old historic black and white photos, including the wedding photo of Mr Hodder, who built the hotel. Meals are available both in the main bar and in the dining room and there is seating both under the veranda on the main street or in the small garden behind the pub.

THE WHITE HART HOTEL

Corner Devon and Queen Street, New Plymouth
Built: 1886
Heritage category 1

Occupying a prime corner site in central New Plymouth and built in 1844 as a substantial house, the first White Hart became a hotel in 1859. At one stage used as a military hospital, the hotel became run down and was sold for removal in 1886. What then emerged is now one of New Zealand's most notable historic buildings. Designed by James Sanderson in the Italianate palazzo style, the hotel was originally half the size of today's building. Just before closing time on 11 January 1893, notorious highwayman Robert

Wallath swagged into the hotel and marched up to the barman, declaring: 'Bail up, give me money, for money I'll have. Stand aside or I'll blow your bloody brains out.' Settling for a bottle of whiskey and some bar change, he then rode off on his horse, taking a pot shot at the police station on the way.

Many of the features that now make the White Hart unique were added in the early years of the twentieth century, giving the hotel a distinctive Edwardian style. In 1900 the hotel extensively remodelled and doubled in size; the famous White Hart statue was added at this time. Just who carved the stag remains uncertain as there are two claims: Leo Arden, a young local sculptor, and Mr Andrew of the Whanganui Technical School. Balconies and verandas were added in 1909.

Now the place to stay while in New Plymouth, the demand for accommodation at times was so great that beds were set up along the verandas. In the 1950s a new style of drinking was introduced, where patrons sat at tables rather than stood at leaners. A large public bar was added in 1970, and the hotel then became the city's leading music venue. A little later it became the headquarters for the infamous Magogs motorcycle gang. Renovated and revived in the late 1980s, the hotel finally closed in 2011.

Now at the centre of the Westend Precinct redevelopment, the hotel is a combination of offices and retail. During the renovations, original cobblestones from the 1844 building were uncovered and now preserved. Visitors can still enjoy a drink and food at the stylish restaurants and bars that occupy the courtyard and corner of this great old hotel.

CORONATION HOTEL

67 Bridge Street, Eltham
Ph: 06 764 8039
Built:1902
Food: Good pub meals designed to fill hungry bellies.
Accommodation: Simple clean rooms, recently decorated, with shared facilities.

In a case of prayer giving way to drink, it is ironic that the local Methodist Church was removed to make way for the Coronation Hotel. A grand hotel built in 1902 and named to celebrate the coronation of King Edward VII, the original building had an elaborate parapet and cornice, which at some point in the pub's history were removed for earthquake reasons. Even without this decoration the Coronation Hotel, brightly painted in the Speight's colours and with broad verandas, still makes a splash in Eltham today. While flash out front, the Coronation is definitely more down-home out back, as it still retains the old corrugated iron side walls, a material commonly used for both economy and fire proofing.

Inside, the hotel is typical of a friendly country pub, with a single large main bar as well as TAB and gaming machines. Check out the unique green and red TAB carpet that leads upstairs to the bedrooms, that have access to the wide veranda with excellent views of Mt Taranaki. The hotel was also used during the filming of the 1985 movie *Came a Hot Friday*, starring legendary comic Billy T James.

WAITOTARA HOTEL

1 Kaipo Street, Waitotara
Ph: 06 346 5852
Built: 1871
Food: Simple pub meals.
Accommodation: Four doubles and three singles, with
shared facilities, and a guest lounge upstairs.

Built in 1871 by Captain Thomas Kells, the hotel was located by the river to service the ferry traffic over the Waitotara River. Kells was well ahead of his time by allowing Maori to be served in the bar, a practice not popular with local settlers. The first bridge, constructed in 1874, brought passing traffic directly past the front of the hotel, which then became an important Cobb and Co coach stop. In the 1870s the hotel was described as a building of substance. When the railway reached the fledgling settlement in 1880, the town boomed and the hotel's fortunes with it. Some believe the hotel was burnt down prior to 1900, but no record of a fire exists, though that may not be surprising in an era when fires in wooden buildings were a common occurrence. In the early years of the twentieth century, the exterior was reclad in brick and stucco; most likely as a fire prevention measure, as insurance companies were increasingly reluctant to insure fire prone wooden hotels. After two disastrous fires in 1888 and 1912 at nearby Hawera, companies refused to insure the entire town until a proper water supply was installed.

During the twenty-first century, the population slowly declined, and in 1963 a new bridge bypassed the town entirely.

The hotel's exterior today would still be easily recognised by anyone alive 100 years ago, and it is now the heart of this small community. In much the same fashion as earlier

hotels, the Waitotara Hotel is not only the pub but also the store and the post office. Inside, many of the features of the old pub survive, such as timber floors, wooden wainscoting, a fine staircase and the original fireplaces. The back of the hotel (now facing the main road) has been opened out and extended, and beyond that is a spacious garden. The attractive public bar features a high ceiling crossed by wooden beams on which have been stamped the names of local stations. Curiously, given the height of the ceiling, locals and visitors have somehow managed to add their names in chalk to the station names, making the bar feel very personal.

WHANGANUI

RIVERBOAT BAR AND CAFÉ (AVOCA HOTEL)

448 State Highway 4, Upokongaro, Whanganui
Ph: 06 345 6410
Built: 1929/1931
Food: Country style pub food.

Starting life as Kennedy's Hotel in 1866, the original bar was little more than a plank or two between barrels, though over the years the hotel became more sophisticated, servicing the busy steamer traffic on the Whanganui River. One story tells of a Mexican (yes Mexican!!) bushman, George Laurent, who in 1910 became totally infatuated with a woman then living at the hotel. The woman told the Mexican that she would 'consider' him if he saved a certain amount of money. The bushman toiled furiously, each week giving the woman money towards the grand total. However, when the final total was

reached she still rejected her suitor. With Latin fire he then decided to blow up the hotel (and the woman inside) with gelignite in the early hours of the morning. He only succeeded in blowing out all the windows and scaring everyone in the township awake. Rejected and dejected with failure on both the love and demolition fronts, the forlorn Mexican threw himself in the river and drowned!

The old two storied hotel burnt down in the late twenties and on October 21st 1929, three days before the new hotel was due to open, this building too went up in flames. With the new construction being concrete, the building was not totally destroyed and finally opened its doors in 1931. In 1994, the Avoca was the scene of an armed holdup, and during the drama a shotgun was fired. The holes from the shotgun blast are still visible on the hotel wall today.

Now known as the Riverboat Bar and Café, a large, enclosed deck has been added across the front of the old hotel, opening up the building to the river and the afternoon sun. Upokongaro is the destination of the river boat trip up from Whanganui. More recently the opening of the cycle bridge and the creation of cycle paths along the river have made the township and the pub a popular spot to take a break.

THE GRAND HOTEL

Corner Saint Hill and Guyton Streets, Wanganui
Ph: 06 345 0955
Web: www.thegrandhotel.co.nz
Built: 1927
Heritage category 2
Food: The Grand hosts a Breakers Bar and Restaurant, with a surf theme, clean modern lines and a standard menu of classic dishes.
Accommodation: 58 en suite rooms that include a 'new' wing built in the 1960s. The rooms are clean, quiet and have off-street parking.

Large, imposing and sprawling across a corner site, this substantial hotel was built in 1927 by well-known identity George Spriggens, and modestly named the Spriggens Grand Hotel. Five years later, Spriggens sold the hotel and the Spriggens name was dropped to become the Grand Hotel. In 1951 Thomas Hurley purchased the hotel, which then stayed in the family until 1987, but the name changed yet again to Hurley Grand Hotel. This is the hotel where the important visitors stayed when they visited Whanganui, and the hotel still has the security plans for the visit of then-Prime Minister Robert Muldoon, who stayed at the Grand during a visit to the city.

Now known as the Grand, the hotel is fortunate in retaining its original exterior and a superb, highly ornate foyer and dining room (the 1967 is extension is behind the building). A wide wooden staircase winds up from the foyer to the first floor, past the original leadlight windows, while in the spacious dining room the intricate plasterwork on the ceilings and pillars has been restored to its former glory.

The main dining room has retained its fine decoration from the 1920s and is now used for functions. On the corner is a popular Irish bar and, in complete contrast, the 'surf's up' Breakers Bar and Restaurant takes up the ground floor along Guyton Street. Still a work in progress, old hotels might be stylish and appealing, but they are demanding and expensive to restore and maintain.

THE RUTLAND ARMS INN

48-52 Ridgway Street, Wanganui
Ph: 06 347 7677
Web: www.rutland-arms.co.nz
Built:1904
Food: Innovative gastro pub meals with a small but select wine list and craft beers on tap, matched by friendly staff.
Accommodation: En suite rooms that are spacious and beautifully appointed with the finest furniture and linens. Not for the budget-minded, but well worth it for that special occasion.

Central Wanganui once boasted 26 hotels and today just two remain, the oldest of which is the Rutland, which has been on this site for over 160 years. More than most hotels in New Zealand, the story of the Rutland is one of fire and renewal. The original Rutland was built in 1849, only to be destroyed by fire in 1868. The new and larger hotel succumbed to fire in 1880, and the hotel that replaced it went up in flames in 1903. Rebuilt in 1904, this time in brick, the new Rutland was a grand affair, three storeys high and topped by a turret, and containing 70 rooms, along with shops and offices on the ground floor. Fire again hit the hotel in 1946, destroying the third floor and the turret, which were never replaced. Closed in 1986, the Rutland was saved from demolition in 1992, with part of the hotel revamped as shops and offices in the Rutland Centre, and a restored hotel rising phoenix-like on Ridgeway Street.

The Rutland today is utterly charming and reflects an incredible attention to detail. An intimate bar and restaurant harks back to the Victorian era; the walls lined with old photos, porcelain and decorative relics from the past. Behind the hotel is a courtyard

for quiet outdoor dining, shaded in summer by a large tree. Upstairs the bedrooms are tasteful and luxurious, combining comfort with elegance. Let's hope that the Rutland is preserved from flames for a long future.

MANAWATU

DENBIGH HOTEL

50 Manchester Street, Feilding
Built: Around 1904
Ph: 06 323 9653
Heritage category 2
Food: Classic pub meals and snacks.
Accommodation: Mix of en suite and shared facilities, clean and tidy.

The early years of the Denbigh Hotel in Feilding are a bit cloudy. Local historians date the hotel from 1873, but a report in the *Wanganui Herald* in May 1876 describes the hotel's opening in glowing terms: 'The hotel presents and imposing elevation, having a noble balcony over the veranda on the hall-door site towards Manchester Street and a grand façade on the side facing Fergusson Street.' The hotel was initially for accommodation only and did not obtain a license for alcohol until 14 years later. It may not have sold beer, but the Denbigh had its own sales yards and conducted the first sale of livestock in May 1880, the beginning of the Feilding Sales Yards, still one of the largest and most important in New Zealand.

The timber hotel burnt down in 1904 and the new hotel, the one we see today, was more solidly constructed by the well-known local builder, William Wilkinson, though this hotel in turn was again badly damaged by fire in 1919.

The Denbigh today retains its Edwardian exterior and is barely altered from a photograph taken in 1951. The main entrance has the original staircase and stained-glass windows. A single long bar and dining area runs along Fergusson Street and has recently been thoroughly renovated as the Stockyard Bar and Restaurant, winning the Feilding District's Award of Excellence in 2017. Retaining the original wooden floors, decorated with hunting and farming memorabilia, and with an open fireplace, this light and spacious bar is both sympathetic to the past and modern at the same time.

HALCOMBE TAVERN

15 Stanway Street, Halcombe
Ph: 06 328 8852
Built: 1894
Heritage category 2
Food: Hearty pub meals on Friday and Saturday nights.

Settled primarily by German and Scandinavian immigrants, Halcombe thrived after the railway was built in 1877 and in 1890 had a population of around 2,500. Boasting five churches, four schools, a post office, a bank and numerous stores, the town didn't have a pub until the local boarding house burnt down and was replaced by a hotel in 1894. Steadily the population declined in favour of the thriving settlements of Marton and Feilding, and while the churches, shops and schools have long gone, the Halcombe pub, a tavern since 1992, has survived.

Little altered on the outside, the interior is now a single large bar on the once busy corner, and is very much a local pub. Photos of the Halcombe rugby team take pride of place above the bar, a fine long slab of polished macrocarpa. It's impossible to miss the hundreds of caps that line the walls around bar. The first was a red QEB cap, casually flung at a stag head high on the wall, where it caught on the antlers. Being too high to retrieve, the cap stayed there. The cap's owner, a 28-year-old man, died tragically of a sudden heart attack several weeks later. Not having the heart to remove the cap, the locals (and now visitors) have over the years added their caps as a tribute to the young man; today around 500 caps line the pub walls.

THE EMPIRE HOTEL/THE COBB HOTEL

528 Main Street, Palmerston North
Ph: 06 357 8002
Web: www.thecobbhotel.co.nz
Built:1895
Food: Good hearty pub food at very reasonable prices.
Accommodation: 15 comfortable en suite bedrooms
in easy walking distance of the central city.

Dominating the busy intersection of Main and Princess streets, in 1877 this site was the location of Central School, Palmerston North's first school. Moved in 1890, the school

was replaced by the Empire Hotel, only to burn down five years later. The present building was constructed in 1895 and substantially altered over the years, but in 1997 the hotel was extensively restored to its original state by using historic photographs. Somewhat confusingly, the pub is known both as the Cobb and the Empire.

Today the downstairs area is one large bar running along both fronts of Princess and Main, with the polished wooden floors and extensive use of timber creating a warm and welcoming atmosphere in the style of a traditional Kiwi hotel. It can be a bit blokey, but then you can't have everything. The real treat is the upstairs veranda, which has been widened to create a huge sunny expanse from which to take in the sun and watch the world go by.

THE NEW RAILWAY HOTEL

275 Main Street, Palmerston North
Ph: 06 354 3165 (The New Railway Hotel)
Ph: 06 354 5037 (Railway Hotel Backpackers)
Built: 1904
Food: Good pub meals of the deep fried and grilled variety.
Accommodation: Backpackers.

Palmerston North was once a major railway junction and the centre of the town not only had the railway line running through the middle of the Square, but also the main station and shunting yards located in Main Street. The station naturally attracted hotels, and this explains why three of Palmerston North oldest hotels used to stand almost next door to each other: the Masonic (1870) and the Railway (1904) still remain, but the Café de

Paris (1893) was demolished in 2016 after a fire. While the station closed in 1963 and the railway line moved in 1964, the old hotels still remain.

The first Railway Hotel, built around 1892, originally occupied this site, but was replaced in 1904 at the cost of 7,500 pounds. Through the years the hotel has had several name changes, including the Railway Hotel and the Old Railway Hotel. Today, the Upper floors are a backpackers known as The Railway Hotel while the ground floor is a bar and restaurant called The New Railway Hotel.

Restored in 1994, the three-storey hotel retains its fine Edwardian exterior and, though substantially modified inside, retains the old wooden floors and decorated ceilings of yesteryear. Consisting of a main bar running the length of Main Street, the Railway is very much a traditional Kiwi pub and has a dedicated local clientele. An unusual feature is the large horseshoe shaped bar, designed to maximise the number of people being served at any one time. Very common in older hotels, few horseshoe bars have survived into the twenty-first century.

WAIRARAPA & WELLINGTON

WAIRARAPA

THE GLADSTONE INN

571 Gladstone Road, Gladstone
Ph: 06 372 7866
Web: www.gladstoneinn.co.nz
Built: 1936
Food: Open for lunch and dinner, the Gladstone serves excellent food and is particularly well known for its lamb dishes, appropriate in a sheep farming district. Available are Wairarapa wines, including a good selection from nearby Gladstone vineyards. Sunday lunch is especially popular, and bookings are essential.

Established in the 1870s as the Hurunui-O-Rangi Hotel, to service the ferry across the river, the original pub burnt down in 1934. It was said at the time that the locals were more interested in saving the beer from the fire than saving the hotel. The pub was replaced in 1936 by the long, low building that is there today.

Locally known as 'the Gladdy', the Inn is everything a country pub should be and has long been a destination for locals and Wellingtonians alike.

One long bar and the dining room run along the entire front of the pub, and the style is definitely country. Old wooden floors impart a natural warmth, an ancient wool press forms the base of a table and the bar itself is an amazing creation of chequered inlaid wood. In winter an open fire adds to the cosy atmosphere, while in summer you can take your favourite drink or your meal out onto the broad terrace that overlooks a large grass garden, through dense willows and down to the river. The Gladstone has live entertainment on a regular basis and on the first weekend of October hosts the local pig hunting competition, attracting a large crowd.

THE GREYTOWN HOTEL

33 Main Street, Greytown
Ph: 06 304 9138
Web: www.greytownhotel.co.nz
Built: 1860
Food: Gastro pub meals focusing on seasonal dishes,
with daily specials along with bar snacks.
Accommodation: Seven atmospheric rooms upstairs that retain
many older features of the hotel, with shared facilities.

The Greytown Hotel is a rarity in New Zealand; it has never been moved, has never burned down and has never changed its name! Affectionately known to locals as the 'Top Pub' on account of its location at the northern end of Greytown, the hotel was constructed in 1860 and upgraded in 1898, making this the oldest surviving pub in Wairarapa. Very typical of early New Zealand buildings that 'grew' over the years, the hotel has extensions that were added on at various times, creating a range of rooms in differing styles and even with different floor levels. The ugly stucco plastered over the wood in 1956 has now

fortunately gone. The Greytown has two resident ghosts: a cleaner named Mary who took her life in the hotel, and a man who died after falling out of an upstairs window.

Completely renovated in 2009, the Greytown Hotel is the perfect combination of historical and contemporary style. Polished floors, leadlight windows, original fittings, wood panelling and historical photos bring the past back to life, while at the

same time the pub is light, airy and modern. Running along the northern side of the hotel, the main bar opens out to a lovely garden that is especially appealing on a hot Wairarapa summer's day.

This is one of New Zealand's most appealing country pubs and it is well worth a visit.

TOP, MIDDLE AND BOTTOM PUBS

Quite a few pubs describe themselves as the town's 'top pub', but it has nothing to do with popularity. Pubs were often described by their location, as top, middle or bottom. Sometimes it meant exactly that: the top pub was literally higher up the hill, while the bottom pub was lower down (e.g. Coromandel). In other towns the top pub was merely at the north end of the town, such as in Greytown and Winton. In many instances the bottom and middle pubs have disappeared, but the top pub resolutely hangs on to its claim as the top pub. Winton is very unusual in that all three pubs, bottom, middle and top, have survived to this day.

THE TIN HUT

State Highway 2, Tauherenikau
Ph: 06 308 9697
Web: www.tinhut.co.nz
Built: Around 1923
Food: A small but thoughtfully prepared menu, best described as 'country fare' with a focus on fresh local ingredients. An excellent selection of wines is available by the bottle and glass, including a good range from Wairarapa wineries.

Located alongside the historic race course, the pub was first licensed in 1857, a good 27 years before the Wairarapa Racing Club (encouraged by the local publican Robert Rowe) settled on Tauherenikau as the location of its race course in 1874. Mrs Lucas, the wife of the second publican, Robert Lucas, so enjoyed that races that she was interred on the race course, though later she was reburied in the Featherstone Cemetery. The hotel burnt down in 1923 and a small tin hut was built to keep the license going, as at that time a hotel lost its license if business was not resumed within 24 hours. It was this small hut that gave the Tauherenikau Hotel its popular nickname and the name by which it is officially known today, the Tin Hut.

The plain exterior of today's pub belies a stylish, warm interior and a beautifully large garden that adjoins the race course, with horses thundering past the back fence on the three summer race meetings in December, January and February. Tastefully decorated, the spacious bar is complete with comfy chairs and a log burner, while the adjoining dining room is spacious and opens out onto the garden and the racecourse. Especially appealing to the little ones (and the not-so-little) is the collection of domesticated birds in the garden.

THE ROYAL HOTEL

22 Revans Street, Featherston
Ph: 06 308 8567
Web: www.theroyalhotel.co.nz
Built: 1893
Food: Good range of pub meals and snacks in both the main bar and in the separate dining area. Opens early and is an excellent stop for coffee and cake.
Accommodation: Luxury rooms, eight with en suites and three with shared facilities.

Recently restored, today's hotel was built in 1893 and replaced the original 1868 hotel that was burnt down. There are now 11 rooms upstairs and it is hard to imagine that the hotel once boasted 26 bedrooms, as many of these must have been very tiny single rooms. During the First World War the Royal was a favourite watering hole for troops stationed at the Featherston army camp. In the 1940s, to cater for shift workers building the famous Rimutaka Tunnel, the hotel stayed open for 24 hours a day.

Soldiers and tunnellers would have no trouble recognising the Royal Hotel from the street today, but the interior would make their jaws drop. In the modern Royal, the Victorian style is overlaid with contemporary steam punk. There is nothing to dislike about this hotel. The dark décor and polished wood is offset by the ample natural light and sunshine from the substantial sash windows. The attention to detail is impressive. What appears to be huge iron beams studded with giant rivets are actually concrete used to make the building more earthquake-proof. Perfect from the tiled entrance and fine old staircase, through to the superb plaster cornices and open fireplaces, the Royal is well worth a trip over the Rimutaka Hills from Wellington.

MARTINBOROUGH HOTEL

The Square, Martinborough
Ph: 06 306 9350
Web: www.martinboroughhotel.co.nz
Built: 1882
Food: Bistro dining in a beautifully decorated restaurant,
complemented by an excellent range of local wines.
Accommodation: Twenty stylish rooms in the original hotel and adjoining buildings.

This fine Victorian hotel is impossible to miss because it is located in the heart of Martinborough on the corner of the Square; from which radiate streets in the shape of the British flag, the Union Jack. The town was designed by immigrant John Martin in 1879, and many of the streets – New York, Venice, Panama, Cork, Suez – are named after places he visited in his international travels.

When built in 1882 by Edmund Buckeridge, the hotel had 22 bedrooms and three parlours, and it was considered one of the finest hotels in the country. Ten years later, in 1892, Edmund's brother Robert built the rival Club Hotel on the opposite site of the Square, though this pub has not survived.

The fine, two-storey wooden building with its broad verandas is largely true to the 1882 original and was immaculately restored as a boutique hotel in 1996. Polished floors, elegant lighting, a grand staircase, historic photos and memorabilia together create a stylish yet relaxed atmosphere, attracting locals and visitors alike. An airy corner bar opens out onto the Square and Kitchener Street, and it's the ideal spot to watch the world go by. Behind the hotel is a stunning garden, perfect for that long drink in the afternoon sun.

LAKE FERRY HOTEL

2 Lake Ferry Road, South Wairarapa Coast
Ph: 06 307 7831
Web: www.lakeferryhotel.co.nz
Built: 1919
Food: Dinner, lunch and bar snacks. Gastro pub with a strong
emphasis on fresh fish, including flounder and whitebait.
Accommodation: En suite and shared facility rooms as well as cabins.

In 1851 a ferry service was established to service people traveling from Wellington to Wairarapa along the coast. At the same time, a small hotel, most likely not much larger than a hut, was set up to supplement the meagre income of the ferryman; thereby making this hotel the oldest in the Wairarapa. The original building has long gone, and little is known about the subsequent hotels (two of which burnt down), though the existing building dates from 1919. Right inside the front door are two distinct sections of wooden

flooring, providing the blueprint for one of the early buildings. Later extensions and alterations confuse the picture even more.

Right at the end of the road, overlooking Lake Onoke and Palliser Bay and directly facing the Southern Ocean, this hotel is without a doubt in a unique spot. Both the scenery and the weather are dramatic, and this pub is an ideal destination for getting away from it all. Taking advantage of the location, the bar and dining area are spacious and open, with huge windows and an expansive deck and garden, all with the spectacular views. The wooden floors, open fireplace and friendly service make this hotel well worth the journey, whatever the weather.

WELLINGTON

THE BACKBENCHER PUB AND CAFÉ

34 Molesworth Street, Thorndon
Wellington
Ph: 04 472 3065
Web: www.backbencher.co.nz
Built: 1917
Heritage category 2
Food: An extensive menu offering a range of contemporary and
traditional dishes, most of which are named after current politicians.

Originally called the Wellington Hotel, the exterior of the hotel has changed little and it would still be easily recognised by anyone strolling across the road from Parliament in 1917, when the pub was built. Then as now, the pub is a favourite watering hole for politicians, political journalists, ministerial employees and workers from nearby offices. Nicknamed the 'Puppet's Pub', the star attraction of the Backbencher is the collection of enormous satirical puppets of politicians, sports personalities and famous characters that adorns the walls. If that is not enough, the pub is also well-known for its extensive collection of original political cartoons, that in their own way document the vagaries of New Zealand politics over the last 30 years.

While the decoration is entertaining, the Backbencher is a great place to eat and drink in its own right. The front bar has a busy restaurant serving good 'Kiwi food', while at the back is a sort of sports bar. Both bars, despite the high-profile location, have a friendly, down-to-earth atmosphere. The pub tends to be most busy after work and is packed on nights when there is an event at the nearby stadium.

THISTLE INN

3 Mulgrave Street, Wellington
Ph: 04 499 5980
Web: www.thistleinn.co.nz
Built: 1866
Heritage category 1
Food: Lunch and dinner. Definitely gastro pub food, with prices to match.

Built by Scotsman Thomas Couper, who clearly named the hotel after his homeland's national symbol, the Thistle Inn holds New Zealand's second liquor license. The first hotel was built in 1840 on a rise above a beach and like so many wooden hotels burnt down. Rebuilt in 1866, the Thistle externally has altered very little since, though now it is a fair way from the sea and today has modern high rise buildings as neighbours. Early patrons could arrive at the pub by water and legend has it that the famous fighting chief Te Rauparaha on occasions landed his waka on the beach below the pub for a drink at the Thistle. A poem by Katherine Mansfield about the Thistle hangs on wall and the following quote is the opening line of her 1907 short story *Leves Amore* 'I can never forget the Thistle hotel. I can never forget that strange winter night.'

Renovations have placed considerable emphasis on the historic nature of the hotel with old photos that include great snapshots of many old Wellington pubs that have long since been demolished. Other photos show the Thistle when it was a waterfront hotel and in the foyer are the original plans of the building. A glass window has been inserted into the old wooden floors giving a peek into the old beer cellar below.

Today the pub is one single bar and dining area along with a small sheltered courtyard and can be busy at lunchtimes and just after work. Adjoining the old hotel is an extension containing the hotel's elegant restaurant. The atmosphere is warm and friendly, with a good selection of New Zealand beers on tap and excellent food.

GREAT ART DECO HOTELS OF WELLINGTON

Like elsewhere in the world, New Zealand in the late 20s and 30s was swept up in the art deco fashion, and it was fitting for the capital city that any grand hotels should be built in the new style. Three major hotels were constructed in the period and all three survive, but only just.

The first to be built was the St George Hotel, right in the heart of the city overlooking the busy Willis and Manners Streets intersection.

An older hotel, the Albert, was demolished in 1929, and in its place at the cost of 100,000 pounds rose a superbly modern hotel designed by William Prouse, who was also responsible for the Majestic Theatre a little further north on Willis Street (the hotel was originally to be called the Majestic Hotel). It was constructed of reinforced concrete with a steel frame, a technique that was proven to resist earthquakes in Japan and San Francisco.

Opened in 1930, the St George was the largest hotel in New Zealand, and the design and fittings were hailed as the last word in fashion. Hosting the rich and famous, the Beatles stayed in the hotel during their 1964 tour and huge crowds besieged the hotel, blocking Willis and Manners Streets.

Now providing student accommodation, the St George is a Heritage category 2 historic building and on the ground floor a stylish modern bar, the George, continues the hotel's hospitality tradition.

On 11 October 1937 the Hotel Waterloo opened on the corner of Waterloo Quay and Bunny Street, to provide for travellers at the new Wellington railway station which was then, and still is, the busiest station in the country. Designed by architect Cyril Mitchell and costing 75,000 pounds, the podium and tower building with geometric decoration was art deco at its height. In contrast the Railway Station is an example of the beaux arts style more fashionable in the 1920s. Extensive use of chrome, quality fittings, and stylish bars and dining rooms made the Waterloo the place to stay during the 1940s and 1950s, and it hosted Queen Elizabeth on her tour of New Zealand in 1953. Substantial alterations occurred in the 1960s and 1970s, but gradually the Waterloo fell out of favour and closed in the late 1980s. Classified as a Heritage category 2 historic building, the Waterloo began a new chapter when it reopened in 1991 as the backpackers hotel, which it still is today.

Time has been less kind to the third great art deco hotel: the City Hotel on the corner of Kent Terrace and Majoribanks Street. Designed by the notable Wellington architect Francis Herbert Swan and opened in 1939, the City Hotel followed the sharp, severe lines of art moderne, a style more common during the depression years. Long since closed as a hotel and converted to office space, the building still exhibits a fine period exterior, somewhat marred by the modern top storey added later.

THE SHEPHERDS ARMS HOTEL

285 Tinakori Road, Thorndon, Wellington
Ph: 04 472 1320
Web: www.shepherdsarms.co.nz
Built: 1870
Food: Gastro pub food.
Accommodation: 14 boutique rooms combining historic detail with modern facilities.

Located in the heart of historic Thorndon, the Shepherds Arms has undergone several name changes and transformations since it was established in 1870 at the terminus of coaches travelling from Karori to Thorndon. Always a popular local, older Wellington residents familiar with the 'Western Park Tavern' would likely not recognise the current building, as today the hotel has reverted both to its original name and the architectural style of the first Shepherds Arms.

Offering boutique accommodation within walking distance of the city, the heart of the hotel is a large open bar and restaurant, warmly decorated and with historic photographs and memorabilia lining the walls. The bar opens out to a sheltered north-facing deck; a very popular spot to while away the hours and watch world go by. Friendly and inviting, the Shepherds Arms is an ideal spot to end up after a walking tour of Thorndon or after a long ramble in the Botanic Gardens.

HOTEL BRISTOL

131-133 Cuba Street, Wellington
Ph: 04 385 1147
Web: www.hotelbristol.co.nz
Built: 1909
Heritage category 2
Food: Good hearty pub food and snacks at reasonable prices.

Edwardian in style and dating from 1909, the Hotel Bristol was once a good deal larger, extending up Cuba Street to include the corner with Ghuznee Street. Built by C. London, the London family owned the Bristol until the mid-1990s. However, the main part of the hotel was demolished in around 1970 and the building now known as the Bristol was originally an annexe. A student pub crawl map from the 1960s shows 50 hotels in central Wellington, of which less than 10 remain today, including the Hotel Bristol.

Located in the heart of Cuba Mall, the Hotel Bristol is a popular venue and consists of two huge bars on two levels. Upstairs is the poolroom, while down stairs is dedicated to eating and drinking, with tables and chairs spilling out into Cuba Mall. Thoroughly renovated, the two levels occupy a single large space opened right back to the roof. Many of the key historical features remain, including the old floors and even an original fireplace marooned halfway up a brick wall. The result is stylish and friendly, and it is not hard to see why this is such a popular destination for a night out. The Bristol also has an established reputation as a leading blues venue.

NAUMI STUDIO WELLINGTON/ PEOPLE'S PALACE

213 Cuba Street, Wellington
Ph: 04 913 1800
Web: www.naumihotels.com
Built: 1907
Heritage category 2
Accommodation: 116 Boutique rooms

Today the automatic assumption is that all hotels will serve alcohol, but in the late nineteenth and early twentieth centuries temperance hotels were not unusual. Of the temperance hotels, the most prominent were the Salvation Army's People's Palace hotels. Of the three in New Zealand, in Christchurch, Wellington and Auckland, the Cuba Street building is the only one to survive. The purpose of such hotels was to provide cheap and alcohol-free accommodation, along with religious instruction for the 'fallen and suffering brothers and sisters', and to 'rescue outcasts'.

Designed in the Edwardian Free Classical style and built in 1907, The People's Palace Hotel opened in 1908. A substantial building with 98 bedrooms and one enormous dining room on the ground floor, a new wing was added in 1916. In the late 1940s, the hotel changed its name to the Railton Hotel, but continued to be operated by the Salvation Army until 1986 when the building was sold and became a backpackers called the Trekkers Hotel.

From that low point, things began to look up when in the tradition of many historic hotels, the buildings were extensively remodelled in 2003 as the mid-market Comfort and Quality Hotel. Now refurbished yet again, the old People's Palace is now the boutique Naumi Studio Wellington notable for its unique style and eclectic décor.

SIX O'CLOCK CLOSING

When six o'clock closing for the sale of alcohol was introduced in New Zealand in 1917, it was seen as short-term wartime measure. However, the temperance movement at that time was at its most powerful, and the temporary measure became permanent in 1918. A public referendum was held in 1949, and surprisingly voted to maintain the closing time at 6pm. The law was finally changed after another referendum in 1967 voted to open bars until ten o'clock.

New Zealand was not alone in introducing six o'clock closing. Across the Tasman, South Australia, New South Wales, Victoria and Tasmania all passed similar wartime laws to close the pubs at 6pm, though oddly Queensland introduced 8 o'clock closing well after the war, in 1923.

THE CAMBRIDGE ESTABLISHMENT/ CAMBRIDGE HOTEL

28 Cambridge Terrace, Te Aro, Wellington
Ph: 04 385 8829
Web: www.hotelsone.com
Built: 1930
Heritage category 2
Food: A good range of hearty pub meals.
Accommodation: 62 rooms, a mixture of en suite, shared facilities and backpackers.

Sometime between 1873 and 1881, the first wooden hotel was erected on broad Cambridge Terrace. A fine hotel for the time, by the end of the 1920s it was decided to demolish the old Cambridge and start anew.

The new hotel opened in 1930 and was designed by John Sydney Swan, who near the end of his career favoured the classical style over the fashionable art deco. Patronised by the elite of the city, the Cambridge hosted Queen Elizabeth and her entourage during the 1963 royal tour.

Now on the fringes of the central city, Cambridge Terrace was once an important shopping street. The original hotel had seven retail shops opening on the street, but as

retail declined and six o'clock closing ended, in 1967 the shops were converted into a large bar, which still exists today. It was at this stage that a ladies toilet was added, a feature not thought necessary previously as women only frequented lounge bars.

Today the Cambridge is the last remaining traditional pub in Wellington city. Running along the length of Cambridge Terrace, the huge main bar is the place to go to watch sport on huge screens, order beer by the jug and eat old fashioned pub meals. If it is a true blue Kiwi bar you are after, this is it.

SOUTH

ISLAND

TOPHOUSE
EST 1887

VACANCY

MARLBOROUGH, KAIKOURA & NELSON/TASMAN

MARLBOROUGH

THE TROUT, CANVASTOWN

SH 6, 10 km west of Havelock
Ph: 03 574 2888
Built: 1904
Food: Good pubs meals at reasonable prices.
Accommodation: The hotel has self-contained units and a small area for camper vans behind the pub.

On the road from Blenheim to Nelson where the Wakamarina River joins the Pelorus River, Canvastown is little more than a blink of the eye and the local pub is the only building of significance. A clue to the past is in the villlage's name as here, in 1864, gold was discovered, and overnight thousands of miners descended on this valley. However, the gold rush was fleeting, and within two years the easy gold was exhausted, though dredges continued to work the area for a further 50 years.

Replacing an older hotel, the Pelorus Hotel opened in 1904, and was an important stop on the coaching route between Nelson and Blenheim as well as serving the remnants of the mining community. In the 1960s the name changed to the Trout and when faced with closure in the 1990s, the local community provided the finance to keep the pub open. A firm favourite with both locals and travellers, the Trout is a comfy country pub with its eclectic décor and friendly service.

GROVETOWN HOTEL

2470 SH 1, Grovetown, Blenheim
Ph: 03 578 5525
Built: 1915
Food: The excellent, Japanese inspired menu will
surprise even the most jaded taste buds.

Built sometime in the early 1860s, the original hotel not only brewed its own beer under
the label Big Bush Brewery but also ran a malt house and an abattoir. Destroyed by fire
in June 1915, the new hotel was established on the other side of the railway line, but later
moved back across the railway line and the main road to its present position. Like many

old pubs, there have been numerous extensions, with the oldest part of the pub to the left of the main door.

Typically rustic on the outside, the interior of the pub is quite a surprise and one of Marlborough's hidden secrets. Traditional elements such as the wooden floors, the occasional deer head, old dusty bottles and vintage radios mix with contemporary Maori art and the stylish Japanese restaurant. Adding to the surprise is a large sunny garden behind the hotel, which includes a section with exotic Japanese herbs and vegetables as well as a children's play area easily visible from the main dining room.

Popular with locals, the bar offers a good variety of craft beer and an extensive wine list, which as you would expect has a focus on local labels. The pub is on a very busy road and for safety reasons it is best approached from the south.

RENWICK ARMS COUNTRY CLUB

92 High St, Renwick
Ph: 03 572 8597
Built: 1882
Food: Bar meals and evening roasts.
Accommodation: Five upstairs queen size rooms with shared facilities.

Affectionately known by the locals as the 'Top Pub', the Renwick Arms was built around 1882. After serving the Renwick Township for many years and suffering the scars of a fire in the late 1950s, its license was cancelled and transferred to the Springlands Tavern. It then sat empty and neglected for many years but, after a short time operating as tea rooms and a gift shop, the hotel was purchased by the local community group and reopened as a Country Club.

Many stories have emerged over the years of strange noises and goings on – usually heard at night – such as baths running, babies crying and footsteps on the stairs, convincing many that the Renwick hotel is haunted.

Recently renovated, the single main bar/dining area occupies the corner of the hotel and opens out to a sunny garden bar and BBQ area. The Club hosts an annual fishing competition on the last weekend in February, attracting over 250 entries. Visitors are very welcome and the only requirement is that they sign the visitors book.

WAIRAU VALLEY TAVERN

2692 SH 63, Wairau Valley
Ph: 03 572 2878
Built: 1880
Food: Along with roast meals and pub standards, this tavern also offers Thai food.

Marlborough's most historic hotel can be found just 25 minutes west of Blenheim, on the road to St. Arnaud. The Wairau Valley Tavern boasts the oldest liquor license in Marlborough, issued when the hotel opened in 1856. Destroyed by fire, the hotel was rebuilt in 1880 in exactly the same style as the old building.

Today the walls of the hotel are lined with historic pictures of the Wairau Valley, while an impressive collection of beer handles lines the rafters. A pair of restored wool presses with polished macrocarpa tops complete the picture. A must-stop for anyone travelling on State Highway 63 to or from the Nelson Lakes.

HAVELOCK HOTEL

54 Main Road, Havelock
Ph: 03 574 2412
e: havelockhotel@xtra.co.nz
Built: 1860s
Food: Settlers Restaurant offers a good range of pub meals.
Accommodation: Five upstairs rooms all with shared
facilities, some with views over the harbour.

Originally known as 'Scott's Post Office Hotel' and then the 'Pelorus Hotel', this pub has retained much of its original exterior and the bottle store is believed to be on its original totara piles.

Havelock in the late 1800s was a bustling town servicing both gold mining and timber mills, and directly opposite the hotel are the historic post office and town hall. Stories are told of how drunk patrons rode their horses through the bar or waited until a fellow drinker was completely intoxicated and retied his horse in such a way as to make it very difficult to untie for the ride home.

The main bar, on a busy corner, is light and spacious and leads out to a long veranda with great views over the Havelock marina, the broad Kaituna estuary and beyond to the Mahakapaua hills. The restaurant is decked out with old mining tools and old photos following on with the settlers theme. One of the more recent publicans showed talent as an artist and has painted a mural featuring many of the hotel's regulars.

KAIKOURA

PIER HOTEL

1 Avoca Street, Kaikoura
Ph: 03 319 5037
Web: www.thepierhotel.co.nz
Built: 1885
Food: Naturally fresh seafood and especially crayfish feature on
the menu, along with award-winning beef and lamb dishes.
Accommodation: Nine restored rooms upstairs, with both en suite
and shared facilities and access to the sun-drenched veranda.

Two minutes after midnight on 14 November 2016 a magnitude 7.8 earthquake struck Kaikoura, and those short minutes spelled the end of Kaikoura's old hotels – with the exception of the Pier Hotel, the town's only wooden hotel.

When the wharf was built at Kaikoura in 1881, J.W. Goodall from Stafffordshire England saw a business opportunity and erected the Pier Hotel, with an eye to catch the trade from passing ships and thirsty fisherman. Goodall not only owned the hotel but as the first wharf manager he took a prominent role in local activities, including becoming the town's first constable.

By 1909 the volume of trade was such that a new wharf was constructed, and the hotel was moved to take advantage of increased business. It was cut into three sections and moved on rollers using traction engines driven by Ted Garrett. The first part moved was the front portion, then the kitchen, followed by the billiard room, but the roads were narrow and at one stage a section got jammed. Left behind was the hotel's chimney, which still stands on the original site.

Even before the earthquake it was the oldest hotel in the Kaikoura region and has always been regarded as a fisherman's hotel. It has seen many characters through the years, including Mickey Miskin, who would play piano for hours as long as his glass was full. The exterior is mostly true to the original, though early photos show the hotel having more elaborate decoration.

The view from the hotel over Ingles Bay to the wild Kaikoura mountains is unsurpassed. Huge windows along the front of the hotel make the most of the view and bathe the interior in light and sunshine. Beautifully renovated, the hotel is a wonderful combination of old and new. Historic photos of both the hotel and Kaikoura line the walls. The large dining area is very popular for lunch and dinner, and on a good day service is extended outside and across the road to the grass verge overlooking the rocky shore. Adjoining the dining area is a cosy bar that attracts both locals and visitors.

PUBS ON THE MOVE

With a plentiful, cheap and handy supply of timber, many early New Zealand buildings, including hotels, were constructed of wood. Set on simple wood piles, they were also relatively easy to move, and move they did; in fact some hotels hardly kept still. There were two main reasons for moving. Most pubs that were moved simply followed their customers, and that often meant moving the building when a new railway line went through the district or a major road was realigned, leaving an old hotel stranded in the wrong place. The Towai Tavern, also in Northland, moved back and forth between the road and the railway, and during one shift that lasted three days the bar never closed.

Some moves were innovative in themselves. The Woodstock Hotel near Hokitika was hauled uphill to a site by the new road using beer barrels as rollers. While most hotels that moved were wood, the Hurunui, constructed of limestone, was moved block by block to higher ground after being threatened by the flood of 1868.

The other reason pubs were moved was to replace pubs that had burnt down or been demolished. The Waikino Tavern was twice replaced, first by a hotel from Waitekauri after the Waikino burnt down, and again in 1926 when the area went 'wet' after being dry for 16 years, and in that time the pub had been demolished. This time the hotel came from McKay Town, and was hauled by bullocks over the hills to Waikino in just one day, with the drinks again flowing that night.

NELSON/
TASMAN

THE RIVER INN

20 Waitapu Wharf Road, Takaka
Ph: 03 525 9425
e: waitapu.blast@hotmail.com
Built: 1898
Food: Simple pub meals including what are said to be the best local fish and chips.
Accommodation: Eleven clean and tidy, simple rooms with shared
facilities, backpacker accommodation and camping sites.

Just five minutes' drive from the town centre of Takaka, on what was originally the main road to Collingwood, the River Inn, formerly known as the Globe, was built in 1871. Destroyed by fire in 1896, the building as seen today opened for trade on 8 May 1898. A busy port, the inn serviced the local settlement and the passing trade that arrived and departed from the Waitapu Wharf at the end of the road; a small fishing fleet still uses the port. The railway line that once passed right by the front door is long gone. The local post office was also attached to the hotel, which changed its name to the River Inn in 1994.

A classic nineteenth century hotel, little has changed at the River Inn – even to the point of still sitting on its original wooden piles. The huge main bar, which opens out onto a rustic garden bar, is decorated with hunting trophies of deer and pig heads, and the pub hosts an annual pig hunt for charity. However, worth a visit in their own right are the two impressive totem pole type carvings in the bar, created by local Neil Baker. A lovely open fireplace attracts the locals in winter.

Set in a peaceful rural river setting, the inn is at the gateway to the world famous Waipupu Springs and has bus connections at the door to Abel Tasman and Heaphy Track. Down by the river at the bridge you can swim with New Zealand's largest trout in their natural habitat. Wet suits and mountain bikes are available for hire at the River Inn.

THE TELEGRAPH HOTEL

2 Motupipi Street, Takaka
Ph: 03 525 9445
e: info@thetele.kiwi.nz
Built: 1915
Food: Open for lunch and dinner and serving good honest pub food.
Accommodation: Two en suite rooms, ten rooms with
shared facilities, plus two bunkrooms.

Dominating a busy intersection on the southern approach to the town, the two-storey Telegraph Hotel with its distinctive verandas is hard to miss. Little has changed and the hotel would be easily recognisable by a local teleported from 1915. The first hotel on the site was built in 1883 by James and Sarah Reilly. Betraying his background, James was widely known by his nickname 'Shamrock'. Later, with their son James Jr, the Reillys built the nearby Junction Hotel, which was demolished in 2015.

Built of untreated totara and matai, by 1914 the old hotel was thoroughly rotten and, as the saying goes, all that kept the building standing was 'the borers holding hands'. Not long after the local council had insisted that the Telegraph Hotel needed major renovation, on Show Day in January 1915, the old hotel went up in flames.

While the road frontages of the new hotel were wood, the rest of the hotel was corrugated iron; partly for economy but also as a fire prevention measure at a time when there was no public water supply or fire brigade. Up and ready for business by November 1915, the builder, Andrew Miller, was at the same time constructing the Hampden Hotel at Murchison – using exactly the same plans for both hotels. From 1936 to 1974, the pub was run by the legendary Floss Moresby, whose benign ghost is now said to haunt the building.

Today the busy Telegraph Hotel is popular destination for locals and visitors alike. The dining area sits to the side of the hotel with a very pleasant outdoor area, and across a small courtyard is the large public bar with a friendly and welcoming atmosphere and featuring photos of the local Takaka Rugby Club teams.

OLDEST NEW ZEALAND PUB

A continual topic of discussion, it is not easy to track down the oldest pub, or even what constitutes a pub. Many early hotels were mere shacks serving alcohol as well as providing very basic lodging, and licensing wasn't a legal requirement until after 1840.

The old wooden hotels burnt down with alarming regularity, often more than once. With the earliest permanent European settlement taking place in Northland, this area appears to have the first hotels. The Duke of Marlborough in Russell can trace its history back to 1827, though it has burnt down several times since. The oldest existing pub building, dating from 1833, is the Horeke Hotel in the Hokianga, though it has been extended several times and considerably altered. When it comes to the first licensed hotel, the records are clear. That honour goes to the Duke of Marlborough in Russell, first licensed in 1840, followed by the Thistle in Wellington.

In the South Island it is believed that the oldest pub still standing it the Moutere Inn, north west of Nelson and built in 1850, though it started life as a house and didn't obtain a license until 1857. The Tai Tapu Hotel was built the year before, in 1856.

MOUTERE INN

1406 Moutere Highway, Upper Moutere
Ph: 03 543 2759
Web: www.moutereinn.co.nz
Built: 1850
Food: Contemporary tasty menu – no deep fried chicken bites here.
Accommodation: Three upstairs rooms with shared facilities and one with en suite.

Tucked away from the main road and not so easy find, the Moutere Inn retains its Old World Pub feel, but is eminently stylish at the same time. Built in 1850 by German settler Cordt Benseman, very little of the exterior has changed, apart from tasteful additions in the 1960s, and the building would still be recognisable to Herr Benseman today. Benseman was a leading figure among German immigrants from the ship *St Pauli*, who arrived in June 1843. Later settling in the area known as Sarau, Benseman built a family home in 1850, and in 1857 extended that house and obtained a hotel license. German

influence remained strong until the First World War when Sarau became Upper Motere and many families Anglicised their names.

There is considerable debate regarding the Moutere Inn as New Zealand's oldest hotel, and a framed document hanging on the wall details their claim against other old New Zealand hotels. The inn can claim to have never been destroyed by fire, to have never moved and to have been continuously licensed since 1857.

On a gradual rise, the hotel has a sunny and open aspect both inside and out, with large windows taking advantage of the view. Numerous historical photos of the both the hotel and previous publicans, including Benseman, line the walls alongside facsimiles of letters and documents dating back over 100 years. The hotel claims that it has offered over 400 different beers on tap since 2008 and these are complemented by a wine list that only features wines grown within a 10km radius of the pub. A beautiful rimu bar top completes the picture of the ideal country pub. The pub holds numerous events, from live music to the intriguing Cigars and Whiskey evenings.

TOPHOUSE HISTORIC INN

68 Tophouse Road, St Arnaud, Nelson Lakes
Ph: 03 521 1269
Web: www.tophouse.kiwi
Built: 1887
Heritage category 1
Accommodation: Four stylish bedrooms with shared facilities,
plus four two-bedroom self-contained cottages.

Just nine kilometres from St Arnaud, this is the only surviving guesthouse of a series of similar guesthouses through the mountains that were built to provide basic food and lodgings for travellers and drovers between Nelson, Marlborough and Canterbury. A license for a hotel was granted in 1844 and the original Tophouse was built in 1846 on the road from Nelson to the lakes, taking its name from its position at the top of the Wairau, Motueka and Buller Rivers. Falling into disrepair, a new hotel was built in 1886 by ex-ship's carpenter Ned James, and both internal and external walls are entirely

constructed of cob. There is an exposed section in the hallway that shows the method of building with cob.

Tophouse was the scene of a grisly murder/suicide in 1894, after the brother of the publican's wife fell in love with the governess of the publican's children. It was not a happy ending. On a more cheerful note, Tophouse holds the record for having the smallest bar in NZ. Originally the bar was a cupboard inside the house, until Licensing Commission Laws insisted on a 'proper' sized bar being built in 1926. The owners compiled by an addition at the end of the house made with old packing cases.

Even today the hotel has a cosy and welcoming feel, but it wasn't always the case. Tophouse was haunted by a resident ghost called Sidney (and never, ever Sid!) who disturbed the guests by shaking them awake during the night. Sidney was a tinker who died in the hotel after being thrown from his horse-drawn cart. But apparently even ghosts have their price after a stern talking to and the promise (a promise so far kept) of a slice of Red Leicester cheese for Christmas, Sidney has left the guests to slumber on.

Currently the hotel provides accommodation only.

WAKEFIELD HOTEL

48 Edward Street, Wakefield
Ph: 03 541 8006
Web: www.thewakefieldhotel.co.nz
Built: 1867
Food: Good pub meals at cracking prices.
Accommodation: Six upstairs rooms with en suite and shared facilities.
In the main street of the quiet country village of Wakefield, just west of
Nelson, is the superb historic Wakefield Hotel. Originally built of wood, the
hotel was extensively remodelled in the early years of the twentieth century
and a coat of stucco added, mostly likely as a fire prevention method.

To those who assume that Victorian moral standards were a good deal higher than those of today, it might come as a surprise that many nineteenth century hotels were also run as brothels, usually very discreetly. A photograph taken in the latter years of that century points to the Wakefield Hotel offering just such service. Taken in front of the hotel, at first glance the scene is typically Victorian; a number of sober looking folk lined up in front of the hotel and two men on horseback. However, closer inspection of the photo apparently reveals a bare breasted woman peering out from an upper storey window – or it is just two billowing curtains? Drop by the Wakefield, take a look and make up your own mind.

The Wakefield has other claims to fame, as an ammunition storage base during the war years, and much later as the first hotel in Australasia to operate a TAB, though the TAB is now long gone.

Today the hotel is a good deal more relaxed; the walls are lined with old photos, the comfortable bar is warm and friendly, the restaurant offers comfortable dining and the garden bar hosts live music on Sundays during the summer.

WEST COAST

KARAMEA VILLAGE HOTEL

Corner Waverly Street and Wharf Road, Karamea
Ph: 03 782 6800
Web: www.karameahotel.co.nz
Built: 1906
Food: Simple menu including local whitebait fritters;
a bit pricy but the meals are huge.
Accommodation: Nine modern units adjacent to the hotel, three with kitchens
and the remainder en suite. Plus a three-bedroom flat for families and groups.

While gold was discovered in the area in the 1860s, results were poor and the first settlement of the small Karamea plain didn't occur until 1874. In 1876 James Simpson opened the Simpson's Hotel and Accommodation House, which included the post office, with James both postmaster and publican until 1897. When his son William (Bill) Simpson took over

in 1906, he rebuilt the present hotel on the existing site. William died in 1944 and his wife Joanna ran the hotel for another twenty years; his grandson Ross took over the licence in 1976. The hotel had been in the Simpson family for over 100 years.

Diane and Keith Storer took over in 1983, by which time the hotel was a tavern. The Shorers revived the hotel by buying the old postmaster's house next door and turning it into accommodation. In 1997 they changed the name to the Karamea Village Hotel.

Retaining its smart Edwardian exterior, the hotel's interior is modern, clean and tidy, with an old open fire that roars into life in winter to create a warm atmosphere. However, the main bar /dining room is odd. The pool table takes up considerable space just inside the main door, and apart from a few bar leaners, there is nowhere comfortable to sit; the space crowded with dining tables reminiscent of a canteen. The hotel is now a popular stopover for those starting or finishing the Heaphy Track and visitors to the Oparara Basin and Fenian tracks.

NGAKAWAU TAVERN

31 Main Road, Ngakawau
Ph: 03 782 8035
Built: 1927
Food: Good pub meals to eat in or takeaway. Chinese cooking on Thursdays only.
Accommodation: Five period rooms, clean and tidy
and with comfy beds. Shared facilities.

In 1870 William McNarn established McNarn's Hotel on the south bank of the Ngakawau River, to take advantage of the busy traffic travelling to the numerous small settlements as far as the Mokihinui River. The railway line reached Ngakawau in 1877 and for many years Ngakawau was the terminus, until the line was pushed through to Mokihinui in 1895.

Along with the hotel, McNarn farmed fifty acres and created an expansive sports ground adjacent to the hotel, that frequently attracted over 2,000 people to the annual sports day held between Christmas and New Year. His son, also called William, took over the hotel and in addition became the local postmaster.

Fire destroyed McNarn's Hotel in 1927, and a new and much larger hotel was rebuilt on the same site and renamed the Marine Hotel. With a wooden façade and the rest of the building corrugated iron, this hotel has changed little since 1927 apart from a coat of stucco over the timber. Over the years, as coal mining and the towns along the coast declined, the hotel changed names numerous times, from the Marine to the Ngakawau Hotel, then later to the Charming Creek Hotel and now back to Ngakawau.

In the meantime, the sports ground has become the home of the Ngakawau Rugby Club and the hotel has numerous photos of teams dating as far back as 1923. Large windows have been added to main bar and dining room, so the pub patrons have a grandstand view of local rugby games.

Upstairs is like stepping back into 1930, with the stairs, wooden ceiling and doors all dating from that time. Some of the rooms still have scrim wall cladding (scrim is a loose weave sacking material attached to internal walls of wide wooden planks over which was pasted the wall paper).

A small café with a lovely sunny outdoor area operates during the day. Comfortable and friendly, the pub attracts locals and visitors to the popular Charming Creek Walkway.

HAMPDEN HOTEL

42 Fairfax Street, Murchison
Ph: 03 523 9008
Web: www.hampdenhotelmurchison.co.nz
Built: 1915
Food: Something for everyone, with a café offering coffee and cabinet food, and takeaways and restaurant meals available.
Accommodation: Twenty upstairs rooms, en suite and shared facilities.

Downie's Hotel was built by Charles Downie on the corner diagonally opposite the Commercial Hotel in 1900; it later burnt down on 5 December 1914. The present hotel was then rebuilt as a single storey pub and operated under various names, including Ross's Hotel. In 1927 a top storey and cantilevered balcony were added. Two years later, on 17 June 1929, the devastating Murchison earthquake moved the whole building nearly half a metre, but as it was built of wood a system of pulleys pulled the pub back in to position.

In more recent years, publican Robert Hamilton had a frightening experience one day when a gunman entered the bar and demanded he fill his flagon with wine. Robert nervously carried out his instructions, only to witness the villain throw some money on the counter and tell him to keep the change.

Now including a café in addition to the bar and restaurant, the Hampden is the perfect stop on a journey along the Buller River. Recently renovated, the historic photos of the hotel and town are a perfect contrast to chic retro and contemporary furniture. Open all day, customers can lounge in the lovely garden bar with a glass of wine, or relax in the sun in front of the hotel with a good cup of coffee.

OWEN RIVER TAVERN

1569 Kawatiri-Murchison Highway, Nelson
Ph: 03 523 9273
Web: www.owenrivertavern.co.nz
Built: 1928
Food: A mixture of Kiwi and Chinese classics along with coffee and cabinet food.
Accommodation: Three motel units and a camping
ground down by the river behind the pub.

The pub is all that remains of the goldfields town that flourished in the valley in the 1880s, and today it is trout that attracts visitors and not the lure of gold. A tiny pub was first built here in 1888 on a site a short distance from the existing hotel, but that building went up in flames in 1927. A more substantial hotel opened in 1928, but over the years the township faded away until just the pub remained, virtually unchanged. In the tradition of older hotels, the Owen River Tavern is the community centre and the post office, and even doubles as the local War Memorial, with a roll of honour to those who fought in WWII proudly displayed on the wall.

Moving from Hong Kong to the hotel in 1997, the contrast must have been enormous for owners Kim and John Siu. Clearly the lure of trout fishing played no small part, as a photo of John proudly holding a huge fish has pride of place on the pub wall. Hong Kong's loss is Owen River's gain, as the hotel offers a delicious mix of pub meals and Chinese food.

Lined with historic photos and with a toasty log burner overhung with a huge stag's head, the cosy pub also has elements of Chinese style, making the Owen River Tavern a unique stop on any South Island tour.

WILSON'S HOTEL

32 Broadway, Reefton
Ph: 03 732 8800
e: wilsons_hotel@hotmail.com
Built: 1873
Food: Bistro meals available from the bar or café.
Accommodation: Seven older style rooms with shared facilities.

Reefton, nicknamed Quartzopolis, flourished in early 1870s, and in keeping with its boomtown image was the first town in New Zealand to have electric street lighting, just a few years behind New York. Driven by gold-obsessed speculators, investment in local mining companies reached such inflated prices that the market finally overheated and crashed in 1883, causing many companies to fail.

One of the first hotels in the area, Wilson's Miners Hotel was built in 1873 by James Wilson, and following his death run for many years by his two daughters. Now known as Wilson's Hotel, it is the oldest of the surviving pubs in a town that still has many of its historic buildings. This two-storey building still stands proudly at the top of the town, and the main part of the hotel is still original. Only the front is wood, with the rest of the exterior corrugated iron. An extension to the bar and a private bar garden on the northern side was added much later. Warm and inviting, the inside of the pub retains much of its old world charm and still features its grand old chandeliers.

FORMERLY THE BLACKBALL HILTON

26 Hart Street, Blackball
Ph: 03 732 4705
Web: www.blackballhilton.co.nz
Built: 1910
Heritage category 2
Food: A classy gastro pub menu along with lighter meals and
burgers. Open seven days for lunch and dinner.
Accommodation: Sixteen simple rooms with shared
facilities, including bunk and family rooms.

Publican Jass Irvine owned the Junction Hotel, at the foot of the Blackball Hills, but after the construction of the new railroad bridge he built a new hotel up on the terrace and transferred his license. On 1 July 1910 the Dominion Hotel opened for business.

Blackball is one of those unique places in New Zealand where fact has blended with fiction, but there is no doubt that the township has played a special role New Zealand's industrial relations history, and this hotel has been at the heart of it all. The town itself evolved around coal mining and rocketed to fame in 1908 when miners went on strike for three months, aiming to extend Crib Time (lunch) from 15 minutes to 30 minutes. The miners were taken to court and, as they were breaking the law, they were fined for their actions – though in a supreme case of irony the judge hearing the case adjourned the court for a lunch break of 80 minutes. It was from the actions of this strike that New Zealand's Labour Party rose, and it is said that the party was formed in the hotel.

Without a doubt the town was a stronghold of militant unionism, and in 1925 the New Zealand Communist Party moved its headquarters from Wellington to Blackball. Over the years mines have come and gone and, while the town is a shadow of its former self, today it is a flourishing township of over 300 people.

In 1968, under the ownership of Joan Fleming, the license was revoked. The hotel remained unused until a group of rock collectors took over, and this caused the Fire Service to insist upon an upgrade for safety reasons. Proving too costly for the rock hounds, they sold the old hotel to Mike Graham, who gradually restored it.

The current name has a story of its own. In the late 70s the then owners of the hotel changed the name to the Blackball Hilton, a rather tongue-in-cheek name but with strong local connections, as the main street is called Hilton after one of the early mine managers. However, after fierce objection and the threat of legal action by a well-known hotel chain in 1992, the hotel remained nameless for a considerable time until Jane Wells and Linda Osbourn brought the building and merely added 'formerly' to the name, to become Formerly the Blackball Hilton.

Today the large two-storey wooden hotel is a destination in its own right and attracts a constant stream of visitors both from New Zealand and around the globe. Crammed with memorabilia and old photos, mostly related to the labour movement in New Zealand, the walls covered in newspaper clippings are fascinating reading. One wall features a special memorial to the men who died in the Pike River mine. Outside, the famous gazebo, erected well before smoking was banned, is still a haven for smokers. Recently renovated, the dining room as been extended and a garden bar added, but the hotel still exudes an old world charm.

The pub host numerous events, including an annual pool tournament, the Pike River Memorial Bike Run and the Blackball Blast.

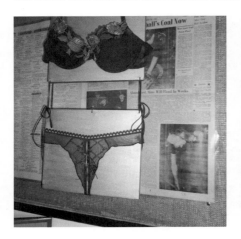 

NELSON CREEK HOTEL
(COMMERCIAL HOTEL)

624 Nelson Creek Road, Nelson Creek
Ph: 03 732 4845
e: jackieandneville@outlook.co.nz
Built: 1930s
Food: Simple pub food with a focus on burgers.
Accommodation: Three rooms with shared facilities plus a bunk room.

Despite the signs and the popular t-shirts bearing its name, officially Nelson Creek Hotel doesn't exist and never has. Built in the mid-nineteenth century, the hotel was then and is still now the Commercial Hotel. Some years ago a beer company took down the Commercial Hotel sign in order to replace it with a new sign advertising beer, to which the words 'Nelson Creek' were added to indicate the location. The old sign was never replaced and over the following years the hotel gradually became known as the Nelson Creek Hotel, or by locals as just plain 'the Nelson', and the real name of the hotel was quietly forgotten. Recently the current owner discovered the old Commercial pub sign on a neighbouring property and has plans to restore the sign, though the pub will still be known as the Nelson Creek Hotel.

Gold was discovered here in 1865, and immediately 1,200 miners descended on the area to try their luck. The main workings were directly across the road from the hotel and on the opposite bank of the creek, which was stripped bare of any vegetation by vigorous sluicing. However, finds were patchy, and by 1901 just 36 people lived at the settlement, though at one point eight gold dredges operated along the creek and had considerably better luck extracting gold than the early miners. To some extent timber replaced gold, but gradually both the dredges and the timber mills closed. An old water race built through soft sandstone to take water to the workings still runs under the road from the hotel. The popular DOC walkways through the historic mine workings start in the reserve over the road.

In the 1930s fire struck the hotel and destroyed the front part of the building, so today the front of the hotel has a distinctive 1930s look, while the back half is much older. One of the early publicans, John Tobin, still has relatives living in the township.

Typical of the smaller West Coast hotels, most of which are long gone, the Nelson Creek Hotel has a small front bar and limited accommodation out back. It is a friendly place where the locals are happy to strike up a conversation with visitors, and if darts are your game make sure you drop by on a Saturday afternoon.

THEATRE ROYAL HOTEL

81 Seddon Street, Kumara
Ph: 03 736 9277
Web: theatreroyalhotel.co.nz
Built: 1876
Food: Catering for breakfast, lunch and dinner, the focus is on simpler, lighter meals – with whitebait fritters a house speciality – and a good wine list to match. Coffee and cabinet food is available for those short on time.
Accommodation: Nine historically themed rooms with en suites, as well as two cottages.

One of this country's last gold rushes, gold was discovered at Kumara in 1876, and by the end of the year the Theatre Royal Hotel was up and open for business. Catering to the thousands of miners pouring into the area, Annie and Otto Anderson (she was from Germany and he was from Scandinavia) did much more than just provide bed and dinner. Flush with gold, their customers wanted entertainment and women, and that's exactly what the Andersons provided. International acts travelling the goldfields of the world performed at the hotel, along with local personalities, including the local Member of Parliament, Richard Seddon, who sang in the hotel's purpose-built theatre. Dancing girls, who worked through the night (the law stated that they should not work later than 6am), danced with the miners for a fee and, of course, also provided more personal services.

At the height of the gold rush, Kumara boasted over 40 hotels, but as the gold ran out so did the town's prosperity.

The Theatre Royal Hotel was abandoned and close to ruin when Mark and Kerri Fitzgibbon bought the hotel and began restoration in 2010. Truly a phoenix rising from the ashes, the reborn Theatre Royal went on to win the HANZ award for Best Country Hotel two years in row, in 2014 and 2015.

Renovated rather than restored, the hotel reflects all the elegance of the Victoria era yet is contemporary and comfortable. A single long bar and dining room runs the entire length of the hotel, and terraces on either side catch the morning or afternoon sun. The polished wood furniture and stone fireplace are enhanced by the perfectly chosen carpet with its busy floral design. Old bottles, plates, photographs and paintings decorate the walls, yet the effect is restrained and interesting, not cluttered.

Kumara is no longer a town to rush through; whether it is good coffee, high tea or something more substantial, the Theatre Royal is an essential stop on any visit to the West Coast.

OTIRA STAGECOACH HOTEL

SH 73, Otira, Arthur's Pass
Ph: 03 738 2890
Web: www.otirahotel.co.nz
Built: 1912
Food: A cut above the average pub meal plus snacks, coffee and cabinet food.
Accommodation: 10 restored rooms, a mixture of en suited and shared facilities.

Situated at the foot of the steepest and most difficult section of the road through the Arthurs Pass, the Terminus Hotel was first built at Otira in 1865. After a flood washed away the hotel and the road during the 1880s, the road was moved higher up the hillside, and naturally the hotel followed.

While the railway line didn't reach Otira until 1900, work had begun as early as 1887. A tunnel was started under Arthurs Pass, and at one point 600 workers and their families lived at Otira. Many of the tunnel workers were heavy drinkers, forming clubs to keep down the cost of the beer, and it was not uncommon for up to forty men to be absent from work for 3-4 days after pay day!

In 1900 two hotels serviced this important coaching stop, the George Dyer Hotel and the Terminus. On 26 November 1911 fire destroyed the Terminus, which was quickly rebuilt with 24 rooms and became the Otira Hotel standing today. Once the tunnel was opened in 1923, the town went into a slow decline; though it continued to house workers crucial to maintaining the very difficult stretch of road between Otira and Arthurs Pass, which was subject to constant slips and washouts. The hotel became a vital stop for motorists needing a calming drink after negotiating the notorious section of the road known as the Devil's Staircase.

Aucklanders Chris and Bill Hennah bought the lease of the land at Otira in 1998 for $80,000, which not only included the hotel but also seventeen houses, the community hall, the fire station and the local swimming pool. A little later they purchased the school. The price is a good indication of the state of the buildings, and while the settlement had a certain charm, it was dilapidated and run down.

In 2010 most of the town, including the rundown hotel, was again up for sale; finally purchased in 2014 by Lester Rountree, a retired deer farmer. Lester began an outstanding transformation of the old hotel, which he renamed the Otira Stagecoach Hotel.

Still a work in progress, the hotel has been largely restored and repainted. Lester, with a great fondness for everything old, has turned the hotel into an Aladdin's cave, with every wall, shelf and floor space packed with period furniture, antiques, collectables and the just plain quirky. Outside are old horse-drawn vehicles and, yes, a stage coach. Renovated bedrooms come with four poster beds and fine furnishings, and visitors can even stay in the room used by Premier Richard Seddon on his regular trips through the Southern Alps. The honeymoon suite is especially fabulous.

Sure, it's a little chaotic, but it's always intriguing and unexpected. Today the Otira Hotel is well worth the stop, but beware, it will be much more than a five-minute stop.

WOODSTOCK HOTEL
(ROYAL MAIL HOTEL)

250 Woodstock-Rimu Road, Woodstock, Hokitika
Ph: 03 755 8909
Web: www.woodstockhotel.net
Built: 1870
Food: Excellent pub food including venison, a choice of steaks, burgers and pizzas.
Accommodation: Four self-contained motel units right next to the hotel.

Once 100 hotels jostled side by side in Hokitika's Revel Street, competing for business during the gold rush era that began in 1864. Hokitika was the main port, but small settlements sprang up all over the goldfields and Woodstock, on the southern bank of the Hokitika River, was typical of such settlements.

When the bridge across the Hokitika River opened in March 1869, Harry Gaylor built a hotel at Woodstock to service the passing trade, modestly naming it Gaylor's Hotel. Further down the hill from today's hotel, the pub was then only the size of the current public bar. When the road was extended south to Ross it was decided to move the hotel 200 yards to the new road, and the entire pub was hauled uphill by cart horses, using beer barrels as rollers. The new location also meant a new name and, as the hotel now serviced the mail coaches travelling south to Ross, the Royal Mail Hotel was appropriate.

Damaged by fire, but never been burnt down, the hotel has had a long, colourful history, and it often doubled as the local morgue. Accidental deaths were common in the mining industry and the custom was to take the deceased back to the nearest public house for an inquest, because the cool cellars for storing beer were also useful for holding the occasional corpse. The mates of the victim would lay out the body for the coroner in the back parlour and sit through the inquest before adjourning to the bar for the wake.

When the railway line was extended south in 1909, the mail service by horse-drawn coach ended, but the single lane bridge handled both road and rail traffic until the 1970s, when new road and rail bridges were built at Hokitika. The loose wooden decking rattled so noisily that the bridge was nicknamed the 'longest xylophone in the world' and the 'clicketty clacketty' bridge. Finally closed in 1978 and then replaced by a new road bridge, Woodstock became and remains a quiet backwater. Much later the hotel name changed yet again, with the addition of the locality Woodstock, though the old name still proudly runs across the façade, a testament to the only survivor in a township that once boasted 12 hotels.

There is nothing shabby about the Woodstock Hotel today. Typical of goldfields hotels, the high façade shields a low wooden building, opening out to the northwest on a wide wooden veranda with amazing views over river, farms, bush and mountains. Liberal use of polished wood for both fittings and furniture gives the pub a warm glow, while the log burner provides real warmth on chilly winter nights. Photos of old lost pubs, most now barely a memory, line the walls, and old bottles along with contemporary photographs and a lively mural behind the stage all add to the atmosphere. Late on cold, windy winter nights a faint spectre of man is sensed at the end of the bar, and although the ghost visits quite regularly, no one really knows who it might be.

The Woodstock hosts regular live music events, and every Sunday the Hokitika Music Club meets at the hotel for jam session that is open to locals and visitors, groups or individuals.

If you need more reason to visit the hotel, the pub is the home of the Woodstock Brewing Company, producing both beer and cider only available at the pub.

Food, music, locally brewed beer, a friendly ghost and a peaceful location overlooking the Hokitika River and the Southern Alps makes the Woodstock Hotel the perfect destination for any visit to Hokitika.

EMPIRE HOTEL ROSS

19 Aylmer Street, Ross
Ph: 03 755 4005
Web: www.empirehotelross.com
Built: 1908
Accommodation: Three rooms with en suites.
Food: Simple pub meals, able to cater for large groups.

When built in 1866, the Empire was one of 21 hotels competing for trade in in the booming gold town of Ross. Today only the City and Empire hotels remain to cater for a township of just 300 people, plus tens of thousands of tourists passing through. The Empire standing today was built in 1908, after fire destroyed its predecessor, and the exterior is a combination of both wood and corrugated iron; the latter material being both cheap and fire proof.

As you step through the double leadlight doors, you enter a hotel that has changed little over the years. The spacious bar would be very familiar now to anyone present on opening day in 1908. What makes this pub particularly special is that the last one hundred years of the local history of Ross has been added to the walls, ceilings and any spare space going. Banknotes hang from the ceiling, historical photos of old Ross line the walls, along with pictures of local sports teams going back 70 years, hunter trophies and even a collection of lumps of coal. Over all this presides a framed photo of Michael Joseph Savage, New Zealand's first Labour Prime Minister. A motley collection of musical instruments is tucked in one corner, just in case the urge to strike up a tune overcomes you. Alternatively you can just stand and warm your bottom by the open fire and enjoy the atmosphere.

If you are looking for a pub with loads of personality, you need look no further.

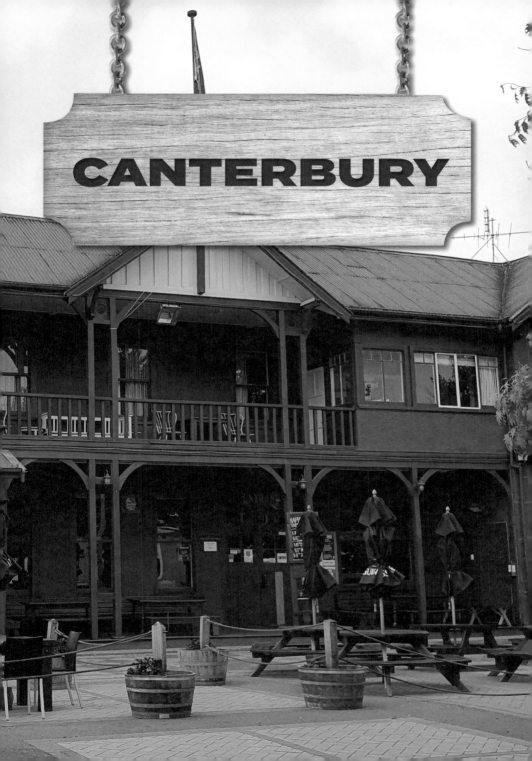

NORTH
CANTERBURY

HISTORIC HURUNUI HOTEL

1224 Karaka Road/SH 7, Hurunui
Ph: 03 314 4207
Web: www.wwwhurunuihotel.co.nz
Built: 1860/1868
Heritage category 1
Food: Country style food with a reputation for generous portions.
Accommodation: Seven rooms upstairs, with shared facilities, plus two five star cottages behind the vineyard.

On the inland route between Christchurch and Kaikoura, the original hotel was built by John Hastie in 1860 on a site near the Hurunui River, and it holds one of the oldest licenses in Canterbury. Named the Hurunui Accommodation House, it was better known as 'Hasties'. The conditions of the license required Mr Hastie to provide eight beds in four rooms, with shelter for up to six horses, stockyards for cattle and fresh horses for those wanting to cross the river, and that he must direct them to the safest point to do so. The hotel served as a central meeting point and run holders would travel from miles around to collect mail and news. Drovers from Nelson would stop here and dip their sheep before crossing the Hurunui River, to prevent scabs from being carried into Canterbury.

After a massive flood hit the region, Hastie's widow decided to move the hotel to higher ground, even though the flood had not directly threatened the hotel. Constructed of limestone blocks quarried from nearby Weka Pass, in 1868 the entire hotel was dismantled and rebuilt on the present site.

In the 1940s the owner, James O'Connell, renamed the hotel O'Connell's Hurunui Hotel. Sadly, as time passed the hotel fell into disrepair, but in 1979 around 100 local shareholders rallied together, and with the help of the Historic Places Trust they were able to return it to its former status. Badly damaged by the 7.8 Kaikoura earthquake in 2016, it took almost two years for the hotel to reopen, in time for its 150th anniversary.

Today the two-storey hotel retains an exterior and interior that reflect a typical nineteenth century hotel. Simple in design, the hotel has a fine façade complemented by a veranda that runs the length of the hotel. Like many hotels of the period, it put its best face forward; the front built with finely dressed stone while the rest of the building is constructed of more basic shaped blocks. Most older hotels have opened up the maze of rooms on the ground floor to form one large bar/dining room, but the Hurunui still retains most of the original floor plan. The main bar just inside the main door is tiny, off which two rooms led to the left and right. Today both are extensions of the bar, but originally they would have been sitting rooms or a ladies bar, each complete with an open fireplace. Beyond, at the back of the hotel, is the dining room. Two garden bars flank the hotel, the one to the left a beer garden and the other a wine garden. The pub runs a small vineyard behind the hotel, producing wine under the Hurunui Village label.

Beyond that wine garden are the stables, which by the year 2000 were in ruin. When the talk turned to restoration, locals returned three truckloads of blocks that had been taken from the stables and used on farms. Behind the stables is the old blacksmith's shed.

And what is an old hotel without a ghost? In this case Charlotte, a maid in the hotel who mysteriously disappeared in the 1890s.

One of New Zealand's most iconic hotels, the Hurunui is well worth the short trip off State Highway 1.

THE PLOUGH

398 High Street Rangiora
Ph: 03 313 7207
Web: www.theploughhotel.co.nz
Built: 1891
Food: An extensive menu, a cut above the usual pub
meals with plenty of options and daily specials.
Accommodation: Six classic bedrooms with shared bathrooms and a shared kitchen.

Solomon Stephens was a man of great energy. In 1861 he built the modestly named Stephens Hotel, but clearly changed his mind as just four years later, Solomon changed the name to The Plough. As well has running the pub, he had a farm on the outskirts of town, where he and his wife Selina lived with their 12 children. But wait, there is more, as Solomon was conveniently a member of the Licensing Committee in addition to the Rangiora School Committee, the local borough council and St John's Church.

Like many hotels, The Plough was a coach stop and it is fitting that the original stables are now located in the middle of the car park.

Fire, the scourge of wooden pubs, claimed the hotel in 1891 and the replacement building, also in wood, still stands today. Over the next 130 years various additions have extended the hotel, but the main building, now restored, still retains all the best features of the original hotel.

Today The Plough is a lively local pub with numerous events including music, quiz and poker nights. The Plough attracted international media in 2016 when the pub banned cyclists in lycra shorts. As one of the owners, Mike Saunders commented: "We get a nice group of customers out here, some elderly folk . . . when you're trying to concentrate on your breakfast you just want to see the sausages on your plate."

OLD LEITHFIELD HOTEL

11 Old Main North Road, Leithfield, Amberley
Ph: 03 314 7230
Web: www.theoldleithfieldhotel.com
Built: 1911
Food: A good range pub meals and bar snacks.

The town of Leithfield, 42km north of Christchurch, is named after the Scottish-born master mariner John Leith, who laid out plans for a town on the south bank of the Kowai river in 1857. The Old Leithfield Hotel, originally called the Royal, was built in 1869 as a coach stop and to service barges on the Kowai River. Directly outside the hotel is a rare example of 'upping stones', a short flight of three steps used to board the Cobb and Co coaches. This hotel was burnt down in 1911 and was replaced by today's building.

Very few changes have been made to the exterior, and inside the pub retains many of the original features, including leadlight front doors, ceiling beams, the staircase and wooden panelling. Extensive use of natural wood gives the bar and dining areas a very cosy atmosphere, a feeling accentuated by the two log burners that warm the hotel in the winter. Historic photos and artefacts decorate the walls. Built on an acre of land, the Old Leithfield is known for the particularly attractive beer garden behind the hotel.

Once on the main road between Christchurch and Amberley, the road and rail now bypass Leithfield, but this is the pick of North Canterbury pubs and it is well worth the very short detour off SH1.

THE ANGLERS ARMS

573 Upper Sefton Road, Sefton
Ph: 03 312 9851
Built: 1905
Food: Good pub style meals that won't leave you hungry.

Today it is hard to imagine Sefton as a bustling port and railway town, and especially hard to imagine the Ashley River handling anything larger than a kayak. Built in 1879 as the Sefton Hotel, the pub serviced both the port and the railway, which reached the town in 1875.

In 1902, the pub had its license renewed on the proviso that a new building was constructed. Opened in 1905 and now christened the Anglers Arms, the same builder was also responsible for two other hotels nearby: the Leithfield Hotel and Ashley Hotel. The similarities to the Leithfield are obvious, but the Ashley at some point had the upper storey removed and now looks very different to the other two hotels.

Now bypassed by road, rail and shipping, Sefton is a sleeping North Canterbury township in which the two-storey Anglers Arms is the most prominent building. Despite a coating of stucco (frequently applied to wooden buildings as fire protection), and in need of a bit of TLC, the outside of the Anglers Arms is largely original. Inside, the cosy main bar/dining area is decorated with memorabilia and old photos, and on the north side of the building is a sunny garden bar. Beyond the garden bar are the old stables, a hangover from the coaching days. A particularly endearing feature of the Anglers Arms is that locals bring in their sporting trophies to display in the hotel.

CUST HOTEL

1709 Cust Road, Cust
Ph: 03 312 5855
e: custhotel@xtra.co.nz
Built: 1863
Food: Pub meals, but the hotel is particularly famous for the pies, made
by the cook affectionately and appropriately known as Cookie.

Built in 1863 (though it didn't obtain a license to sell alcohol until two years later), the Cust Hotel has not burnt down, moved or had a name change in that time and, despite being badly shaken by the recent earthquakes, it has escaped completely unscathed. Located on the halfway point between Rangiora and Oxford, the hotel was an important coaching stop and originally boasted 20 rooms and four sitting rooms. Paddocks were provided behind the hotel for horses, cattle and sheep on the move between farms and sale yards. Ray Dew was the longest serving publican, running the hotel from 1961 to 1985.

In more recent years the old hotel was extended on the western side of the building to accommodate a larger bar, and also upstairs to provide more bedrooms. Part of the hotel operates as an antiques and collectables store known as Done and Dusted. A great little country pub on the road to Oxford, the Cust is a popular with locals, either for a quiet drink or for a meal at Harriet's Restaurant. The bar and dining area runs along the entire length of the building and extends out into wide veranda, perfect for watching the world go by.

CANTERBURY

RACECOURSE HOTEL

118 Racecourse Road, Upper Riccarton, Christchurch
Ph: 03 342 7150
Web: www.racecoursehotel.co.nz
Built: 1883
Food: Hoofbeats Restaurant, open for breakfast, lunch and dinner,
offers a wide range of good value meals, including daily specials.
Accommodation: 46 rooms, all en suite, plus a three-bedroom apartment.

While Riccarton Racecourse was established in 1856, the grey concrete Racecourse Hotel was not built until 1883, especially to service race goers. Said to be one of New Zealand's most haunted buildings, the hotel was the scene of one of New Zealand's most famous unsolved murders. In November 1933 after a party at the hotel, the publican Donald Fraser was shot dead in bed late at night while he lay asleep with his wife. Fraser had a reputation as an obnoxious man who had a violent temper and was a bully involved in shady deals. The weapon, a double barrel shotgun, was never found, and the only clue the police had was that the bullets had been purchased on the West Coast. No one was charged for the murders, as Fraser had numerous enemies and there were too many suspects, many of whom had attended the party and were staying in the hotel. Now his ghost angrily storms through the second-floor of the old hotel, opening and slamming doors, looking for his killer.

Directly across the road from the Riccarton Racecourse, this popular hotel is at the heart of a sprawling complex of bars, restaurants and accommodation. The Hoofbeats Restaurant is a large and busy eatery, and adjoining that is the more refined Carbine Bar (named after a racehorse). Beyond that is the huge public/sports bar, which naturally has a very active TAB. Along the entire front of the hotel are several outdoor areas for eating and drinking.

TAI TAPU HOTEL

780 Old Tai Tapu Road, Tai Tapu
Ph: 03 329 6819
Web: www.taitapuhotel.com
Built: 1856
Food: No ordinary pub meals here, but an extensive contemporary
menu as well as lighter meals and snacks. The food is
complemented by a carefully constructed wine list.

One of the South Island's oldest hotels, the Tai Tapu has never burnt down or moved, though it was originally named the Ellesmere Arms and was an important coach stop on the old road from Christchurch to Akaroa. In addition to catering for the coach horses (the new function centre is on the site of the old stables) the hotel also owned several paddocks to accommodate cattle and sheep being driven to and from the Addington stock yards.

Over the years the pub has had several additions, though the heart of the old pub is still very clearly marked by a substantial beam running through the main bar, which replaced the original external wall. Pride of place is given to a photo of former publican Norman Fisher, then aged just 15. Fisher was a notable boxer who represented New Zealand at the 1936 Olympics in Berlin.

Light and airy, the main bar runs along the north side of the building, with views over green paddocks to the Port Hills. Along the back of the pub is a substantial and attractive dining room, and beyond that a sunny garden bar.

Affectionately known to locals as the 'Tap', this is one of Canterbury's most popular country pubs and is especially popular for Sunday lunch. Make the journey, you won't be disappointed.

GOVERNORS BAY HOTEL

52 Main Road, Governors Bay, Lyttelton
Ph: 03 329 9433
Web: www.governorsbayhotel.co.nz
Built: 1870
Food: Gastro style meals to satisfy all, with blackboard specials and a good wine list.
Accommodation: Seven refurbished rooms with shared facilities and harbour views.

Granted its first licence in 1870 as the Ocean View Family Hotel, the hotel was initially a coaching stop for travellers on the peninsula. Later, Governors Bay attracted huge numbers of day visitors, who arrived from Lyttelton by steam ferry to visit the famous Pleasure Gardens, which covered ten acres behind the hotel. Over the years the pub has since seen many owners, beginning in 1870 with May Haulk, the first publican. In 1903 the hotel was owned by Edward Brownie, an ex prison warden from Lyttelton, who together with

his wife Rose ran the hotel, offering high class accommodation for travellers. However, competition for business was fierce and when the rival pub, the Whitecliffs Hotel, was bought by new owners, it quickly and mysteriously burnt down.

Inevitably the hotel has had its share of facelifts during its long history, and although badly damaged during the February 2011 earthquake, the hotel remained standing, unlike the waterfront hotels in nearby Lyttelton. Recent renovations have enhanced the original historic features and created a unique ambience that blends old and new. Inside, the spacious bar/dining room features the original doors, a double-sided fireplace and wide windows that offer extensive sea views. Outside, a grand upstairs veranda is mirrored on the ground floor by a fabulous terrace overlooking the harbour, unsurprisingly popular on a fine day.

Governors Bay hotel is the perfect stopping point for lunch on a drive around Lyttleton Harbour, and an ideal destination in its own right.

HILLTOP TAVERN

5207 Christchurch Akaroa Road, Little River, Banks Peninsula
Ph: 03 325 1005
Web: www.thehilltop.co.nz
Built: 1932
Food: Everything from substantial meals with a focus on local
ingredients, through to cake and coffee. The wood fire pizza oven
produces tasty fare and keeps the pub cosy through winter.

For centuries travellers have paused at the top of the pass from the Canterbury plains to Akaroa. Maori used this route from the rich fishing grounds at Lake Ellesmere to the great pā on Ōnawe peninsula. Following in their footsteps, early European settlers used the same tortuous route from the plains to Akaroa. A year after a road was opened in 1871, James Garwood built a wooden hotel just below the crest of Barry's Pass as a Cobb and Co coaching stop, and a resting point for drovers moving stock from Akaroa to the railhead at Little River. Destroyed by fire in April 1931, a fine, concrete, art deco style hotel rose from the ashes, and this new pub continues today as a popular stopping point on the journey from Christchurch to Akaroa.

Now a tavern, the iconic pub is famous for its spectacular views over Akaroa Harbour, though on a wet day the tavern is frequently enclosed in cloud. Recent décor reflects the art deco era, with polished wood floors and an open fireplace. An outside dining area is perfect on a fine day. A framed list of all of Hilltop's publicans hangs on the wall like roll of honour. Whatever the weather, visitors can enjoy a lovely warm atmosphere in the stylish bar. Hilltop also holds live music gigs and offers safe transport by arrangement on the peninsula.

MADEIRA HOTEL

48 Rue Lavaud, Akaroa
Ph: 03 304 7009
Web: www.madeirapub.co.nz
Built: 1883/1907
Food: Simple meals at good prices.
Accommodation: Now a backpackers, all rooms are dormitories with shared facilities.

In contrast to most hotels, The Madeira has had few name changes from when it was opened in 1871 by Antonio Rodrigues. Born in Funchal, on the island of Madeira, Rodrigues first arrived in London in 1857 and then set sail for New Zealand, where he arrived in Lyttleton with his wife Adelaide in 1858. Moving immediately to Akaroa, Rodrigues first set up a bakery before working at the Commercial and Criterion Hotels. Finally, he built his own hotel in 1871 and named it after his birthplace. Why Rodrigues came to New Zealand is unclear as, apart from a handful of early Portuguese whalers from the Azores Islands, New Zealand has had very little connection with Portugal. In 1888 he built a small cottage for his family of eight children and this still stands today. After running the hotel for thirty-four years Rodrigues died in 1905 and was buried in St Patrick's Catholic Cemetery. After his death a new hotel was built next door and opened in 1907 with the same name, and both hotels are still standing today.

Akaroa today attracts a huge number of tourists and it surprising that this fine historic hotel with its handsome exterior and many original features, is now run as a backpackers and a fairly modest one at that. A bar at the back of the building is pleasant enough and particularly appealing is the outdoor areas that runs along the northern sunny side of the hotel.

THE GRAND HOTEL

6 Rue Lavaud, Akaroa
Ph: 03 304 7011
Web: www.grandhotelakaroa.co.nz
Built: 1883
Food: Waeckerles Restaurant serves a good range of
meals with an emphasis on seasonal seafood.
Accommodation: Nine plush rooms with en suites.

In March 1840, sixty-three French and German immigrants set sail for New Zealand on the ship *Comte De Paris*. Unaware that the British had claimed sovereignty over New Zealand under the terms of the Treaty of Waitangi, the settlers were dismayed to find on their arrival that the Union Jack was raised at Green Point and they were now arriving in a British colony. Despite the change of circumstance, the immigrants decided to stay.

Jacob Waerckerle, a German migrant, was granted the original license for a hotel, which he christened the Grand Hotel. In 1860 he rebuilt the hotel on the main road into the settlement, and renamed it the French Hotel. Waerckerle, always with an eye for an opportunity, was also well known in the area for importing Ka Ka ponies, renowned for their sure footedness on the hills and rough terrain of the peninsula. He became Mayor of Akaroa in 1878.

Clearly fond of name changes, the hotel was called Waerckerle's Hotel when it was one of three hotels on Rue Lavaud destroyed by fire on the same night in 1882, when an arsonist heaped gorse soaked in kerosene against the walls of the buildings. Although they were a reasonable distance apart, the fires all started within a few minutes of each other; the arsonist was never caught, and the intentions of the arsonist remain a mystery.

After the fire, the hotel was rebuilt by Waerckerle's son-in-law, Robert Bayley, who became the hotel's manager when the hotel reopened in 1883 with a name to say it all: Waerclerle's New Grand Commercial Hotel. Finally, in 1918 the hotel reverted to its original name and has remained the Grand Hotel ever since. Extensive renovations were carried out in 1985, but many of the old features were retained, including the staircase, the coal range and the foot scrapers at the entrance. A small room just inside the main entrance was the original bar; beyond that the main bar, complete with TAB, is a very typical Kiwi drinking hole.

SHEFFIELD HOTEL

40 Wrights Road, Sheffield
Ph: 03 318 3804
Web: www.sheffieldhotel.co.nz
Built: 1882
Food: A superb menu that attracts foodies from all over Canterbury for both the quality and the quantity of the meals. In addition, the hotel offers an extensive bar and burger menu.
Accommodation: Camping ground with facilities for campervans and tents, as well as two cabins.

When in 1876 Michael Flannagan took over the lease of Willis's Hotel in Sheffield, things at first went well; but a few years later Flannagan had a major disagreement with the owner of the hotel. Flannagan was so infuriated that he built a new hotel right next door, and in 1882 the doors of the Sheffield Hotel opened for business. A fierce competition ensued through to 1908, when Willis's Hotel closed and became the vicarage.

Long haunted by two ghosts, there had been many sightings of the spectres prior to the Canterbury earthquakes, since when they have not appeared. One shade is that of an unknown older woman, who drifts downstairs and into the ladies bar, though the bar is no longer in use. When an old picture was removed and replaced by a mirror, the mirror mysteriously fell off the wall. A replacement mirror met the same fate, and today the picture hook remains bare. The other ghost, only seen downstairs, is that of man well dressed in Victorian garb and believed to be none other than the first publican, Michael Flannagan, checking that his pub is continuing to fend off the competition.

Mr Flannagan need not worry. Never having burnt down, moved or changed name, today the Sheffield is the only survivor of the four hotels in the small township. The restaurant is beautiful and the table settings stunning, both reflecting an air of elegance and refinement. The generous main bar is centred on a very efficient Canadian log burner, guaranteed to banish the worst of winter chills. Both the bar and the restaurant overlook an attractive garden bar. Off the main highway, it is easy to miss the Sheffield Hotel, but that would be a shame as it is one of Canterbury's best country hotels.

BLUE PUB (METHVEN HOTEL)

2 Barkers Road, Methven
Ph: 03 302 8046
Web: www.thebluepub.co.nz
Built: 1918
Food: All day pub meals and sharing menu in the bar, or more substantial fare in the Blue Restaurant.
Accommodation: Twelve comfortable upstairs rooms, with shared facilities and access to a private veranda with mountain views.

Robert Patton settled in the area in 1869 after he bought 500 acres at the junction of West Coast Road and Waimarama Road. He named the farm Methven after his home town in Perthshire, Scotland. In 1880 Patton built the Commercial and Family Hotel, sturdily constructed with double thick walls packed with earth and tussock for better insulation.

For a time the local Masonic Lodge held their meetings in the pub.

A some point the pub was renamed the Methven Hotel, and later still became the Blue Pub to distinguish it from the nearby Canterbury Hotel, which became known as the Brown Pub. After a fire in 1911 the hotel was demolished, and in 1918 the present one was built on its site.

Retaining the best historical features and reflecting the local farming traditions, today the Blue Pub is one of New Zealand's most iconic watering holes. No smelly, beer-stained carpet or scuffed paint here; the main bar with its stained wood and farming memorabilia is stylish and cosy at the same time. Outside, the street has been pedestrianised and, with extensive outdoor seating and tables, this is the perfect spot to eat and drink on a sunny day. A tad more elegant is dining in the Blue Restaurant, which echoes the hotel's Edwardian past.

The annual multisport event Peak to Pub begins on the summit of Mt Hutt (2086m) and the competitors ski, bike and run down to the Blue Pub at Methven.

THE BROWN PUB
(CANTERBURY HOTEL)

Corner Main Street and Forest Drive, Methven
Ph: 03 302 8045
Web: www.brownpub.co.nz
Built: 1922
Food: Stylish pub food and a takeaway menu.
Accommodation: Ten upstairs rooms, all with shared facilities.

On 15 February 1883 ex constable William Rowse bought a corner section, and by October of the same year he opened his Canterbury Hotel with the following newspaper advertisement: 'W. Rowse begs to inform the travelling public now having opened the above newly erected and commodious Hotel.'

Fire took hold in the hotel on 19 June 1922, and although the local fire brigade used water from an open water race that ran directly alongside the hotel, they were unable to save the building. Undeterred, James McTaggert, the publican at the time, immediately rebuilt the hotel on the same site using an unusual combination of vertical and horizontal weatherboards. On the morning of 2 July 2019 fire broke out in the roof and although the damage was extensive, it was contained and within five months the pub was back in business.

This is a true country style pub, located in the heart of Methven, and it still retains the two bars that were an essential part of every traditional hotel: the large public bar (men only) and the much smaller lounge bar for mixed company, usually those staying in the hotel. While the bars remain, today the atmosphere is completely different, and things are much more relaxed. In the Main Bar at the Brown Hotel you can chat to bar staff across the solid bar of polished macrocarpa wood, enjoy a game of pool, or take in an evening of country music or karaoke. The stylishly furnished Fireside Restaurant and Bar features a lovely stone fireplace and is now the hotel's restaurant, beyond which is a large garden bar.

SOUTH
CANTERBURY

GERALDINE HERITAGE HOTEL
(CROWN HOTEL)

31 Talbot Street, Geraldine
Ph: 03 693 8458
Web: www.geraldinehotel.co.nz
Built: 1906
Heritage category 2
Food: Good range of pub meals at prices that are hard to beat.
Accommodation: Twenty-six rooms, including 16 with en suites and nine with shared facilities, plus backpackers accommodation.

Europeans first settled along the banks of the Orari River in the 1840s, but it wasn't until 1854 that the first bark hut was built by Samuel Hewlings in what is now Talbot Street. Initially named Talbot Forest, the township was called FitzGerald in 1857, but this name was considered to too cumbersome and later changed to Geraldine, a name that finally stuck. Although bypassed by the railway, the town flourished at the heart of a prosperous farming district, and became a borough in 1905.

Little is known of the old Crown Hotel that burnt down in October 1899, but the replacement building, opened in 1906, was a grand hotel in the exuberant Edwardian style of the new century. Just two years later Geraldine, as part of the Ashburton Electorate, voted for Prohibition, and the Crown, like all other pubs in that electorate, closed. It remained 'dry' until 1950, when the Crown Hotel was reopened by the Geraldine Licensing Trust.

On the direct route from Christchurch to the popular tourist destinations inland, today Geraldine is again enjoying a renaissance as a popular stopping point. The Crown has changed little over the years and, while this has preserved much of its historical structure, it needs considerable TLC. Typical of an older pub, the Crown retains a separate bar and dining room and is decorated with relics of the sawmilling days. Its good value meals draw in the locals.

LICENSING TRUSTS

As the influence of the temperance movement waned, many areas voted to go 'wet', but there was unease about a return to an unrestricted sale of alcohol. The New Zealand Licensing Trusts were inspired by a similar institution in Scotland, where local trusts were set up with the aim of providing outlets where 'alcohol could be sold with care and responsibility, with the well-being of the community in mind, through a charitable organisation whose profits flowed back to the community.' A trust has a monopoly on the sale of alcohol within an area, with trust members voted in during local elections and the profits being returned to the community. With appropriate legislation, the first and arguably the most successful was the Invercargill Licensing Trust, established in 1944, followed by Masterton in 1947. The trusts have been run with varying degrees of success and today around 19 trusts are still operating.

WOLSELEY HOTEL

133-137 Temuka/Orari Highway (SH 1)
Ph: 03 615 7154
Built: 1883/1884
Food: Bar meals Friday and Saturday nights only.
Accommodation: Ten rooms catering mainly to truckies.

When it opened, this large hotel had all the trappings of a first-class establishment, with large, comfortable bedrooms and private sitting rooms that commanded a splendid view over the countryside. Unfortunately, in the early 1900s all this came to an end when a boundary change brought the hotel into a no-license district and the pubs closed. The hotel stables across the road fell into disuse and were soon a favourite stopping place for swaggers.

Later reopened, the Wolseley Hotel held its centennial celebrations at the end of October 1984, but there was a great deal of uncertainty as to the exact date of opening; one source had the hotel being built in 1883, while another stated 1884.

Today the Hotel caters mainly for truckies and passing motorists, in the spacious main bar and dining area that runs along the front of the hotel and out to a large garden bar on the north side of the building. Large numbers of old and new truck photos line the walls.

The annual Winchester swap meet is held in the township in early April, bringing an eager bunch of car enthusiasts to this small rural village, and the hotel is walking distance from this popular event. On the pub wall is a photo outside the hotel of the first annual South Canterbury Motor Rally held in 1910. One hundred years late a re-enactment of this event was held in precisely the same spot, and both photos sit side by side on the wall of Wolseley Hotel. The annual Bike Rally in November also attracts up to 1,500 bikers to the hotel.

PLEASANT POINT HOTEL

95 Main Road, Pleasant Point
Ph: 03 614 7605
Built: 1911
Food: Nelly's Restaurant offers a full menu of delicious fare.
Accommodation: Nine upstairs rooms plus a family room.

Of all the confusing hotel names in New Zealand (and there are many), the Pleasant Point Hotel is among the most confusing of all. In 1874 Thomas Watkins established the Railway Hotel directly opposite the Pleasant Point Hotel, which was established early in 1861 by George Gibbs. Then the Railway Hotel, now under the ownership of Francis Nelligan, burnt down and was rebuilt in as Nelligan's Railway Hotel. In 1927 the Pleasant Point Hotel burnt down, never to be rebuilt. In the 1950s Nelligan's Railway Hotel, under the publican James Richardson, changed its name to the Pleasant Point Hotel. Of course, he didn't quite get around to removing the old name off the high parapet, so today the two names remain.

One of the best country pubs in the area, the hotel has kept all the best features of the handsome brick Edwardian pub, both inside and out. The exterior is virtually original and inside much of the old decoration remains, though the old public and lounge bars have been combined into one handsome bar that opens out onto a sheltered courtyard.

The dining room is a treat – period style tables and chairs complement the original doors, panelling, fireplace and windows – and this restaurant is very popular with both the locals and visitors. Another sunny outdoor area is perfect for dining outside on a good day.

Upstairs the guest rooms have all been pleasantly renovated, complete with a friendly ghost nicknamed George in room three.

When the branch line to Fairlie closed in 1967, a 2km section of the track at Pleasant Point was preserved along with the railway station, which now operates as a museum and heritage railway directly opposite the hotel and attracts visitors from around the globe to this small south Canterbury town.

GLADSTONE GRAND HOTEL

43 Main Street, Fairlie
Ph: 03 685 8140
Built: 1884
Heritage category 2
Food: Good substantial pub meals.
Accommodation: Seventeen rooms with shared facilities. The paint is chipped, and the carpet is worn, but it is very clean and tidy. There is also campervan parking.

In 1884 plans were underway to extend the railway line from Albury to Fairlie Creek, and with that news the race was on to see who would open the first hotel to cater for the expected population boom. Records show that the brick-and-stone constructed Gladstone Grand was completed just before the wooden Fairlie Creek Hotel, though both opened in 1884.

When the railway closed in March 1968, the Gladstone Grand directly across the road from the station, like many other hotels in a similar situation, saw a steady decline in business as the population slowly drifted away. However, in recent years the good times have returned to Fairlie, as it is now a popular stopping point on the busy tourist route to Tekapo and Mt Aorangi/Cook.

The fine Victorian façade remains, and inside the lovely old staircase and plaster arches hint of a lost era. There is a large open bar/dining area with a cosy log burner and a bar made from a great slab of polished macrocarpa. The Gladstone Grand is a friendly local bar and welcoming to visitors.

FAIRLIE HOTEL

69 Main Street, Fairlie
Ph: 03 685 8061
Web: www.fairliehotel.co.nz
Built: 1884
Food: Famous for its extensive burger menu in addition to stone grilled meals, the Fairlie offers both dine in and takeaway options.
Accommodation: Ten sunny upstairs rooms with shared facilities.

In the township originally known as Fairlie Creek the first hotel was established by the Hamilton family around 1865, as Hamilton's Accommodation House. Under the ownership of James Paton Lister it became a hotel in 1868, and when Charles Wedderall rebuilt the hotel in 1876 he renamed it the Clyde Hotel.

With the arrival of the railway in 1884 the small settlement boomed, and the license of the Clyde was transferred to the newly erected two-storey Fairlie Creek Hotel, with Thomas Winter its first Publican. In 1892, the town dropped the word 'Creek', and following suit the hotel was simply known as the Fairlie Hotel.

Nicknamed the 'Top Pub', it was owned by the Manaton family from 1927-1964 and subsequently sold to John O'Connor, who owned the pub for twenty years and raised thirteen children there. Neither of Fairlie's two hotels have burnt down, though the Fairlie has had several facelifts over the years. The main bar occupies the corner of the building, and a small café is open to the main street.

ALBURY TAVERN AND INN

State Highway 8, Albury
Ph: 03 685 5910
Built: 1879
Food: Asian style meals available Thursday to Sunday and including lunch on Sunday.
Accommodation: Six rooms upstairs with shared facilities.

Set in rural Mckenzie country, the hotel opened on 23 December 1879 and was the terminus for the railway line from Timaru until the line was extended to Fairlie in 1884. Known as the Railway Hotel, the first publican was Joseph Palmer, an auctioneer from Timaru. Later the hotel was purchased by Frederick J.P. West, who also owned the nearby stone-built Opawa Hotel. West operated both hotels until 1911, when he sold the Railway Hotel and closed the Opawa Hotel, which he then used as his private residence while farming the surrounding land and breeding horses. Today the old hotel, known as the Opawa Homestead, is run as a boutique bed and breakfast.

For 45 years, from 1935 to 1981, the Railway Hotel was owned by Mary Gibson; a pub ownership record for South Canterbury. In 1967 it was the first in the province to obtain a tavern license and was then renamed the Albury Tavern. The comfortable corner bar – lined with historic photographs and retaining its old stained wood walls – is the ideal stopping point on this route up to the Mckenzie country, though it is only open Thursday to Sunday.

GROSVENOR HOTEL

26 Cains Terrace, Timaru
Ph: 03 687 9190
Web: www.grosvenor.co.nz
Built: 1915
Heritage category 2
Food: Pillars Restaurant offers an la carte menu, while more casual meals are offered in the main bar.
Accommodation: Forty-six superior rooms with en suites.

Affectionately known as the 'Grand Old Lady of the South', this hotel was opened on 1 May 1915, replacing the previous hotel built in 1878 by J. Meckle. It was in this earlier hotel that the Canterbury Rugby Union was formed in 1879. Designed by architect Jas Turnbill and constructed by a local company, the Shillito Bros, the new hotel style was high Edwardian and very little has changed on the outside since that time. The original plastered ceiling and three magnificent pillared archways, with decorative shields emblazoned with GH, are in the foyer.

Occupying the entire street corner, the walls of the main bar have been stripped back to the original brickwork (Timaru was known for its high-quality bricks) and the kauri floor, polished to a high sheen, bears the distinctive imprints of fashionable high heels over many years. This bar retains the old footrest running along the main bar, which was designed to make standing at the bar more comfortable.

While the main highway is now some distance away and the hotel is on a side street off the main retail precinct, this area overlooking the harbour was once the commercial heart of the city. Few hotels can claim two visits by Queen Elizabeth, but the Queen stayed here in 1954 and again in the 1970s. For dedicated royalists, it is possible to stay in room 101 – used by the Queen and Prince Philip. The hotel still has the 1954 menu, which featured baked mountain trout and Veuve Clicquot champagne.

Directly across Beswick Street is the old Royal Hotel; built in 1868 and now converted to apartments.

THE WAIMATE

118 High Street, Waimate
Ph: 03-689 1413
Built: 1902
Food: Extensive contemporary menu that changes constantly
and includes vegan and vegetarian dishes.

Dominating the town's main street, the original Waimate Hotel was built in 1861 and it is not certain if this hotel survived the disastrous fire of 1878 which destroyed the extensive forests and put an end to the local timber milling industry. However the wooden hotel did not survive fire in 1902 said to be caused by the publican falling asleep while smoking in bed. The new hotel, now known as Twomey's, was a solid two storey masonry structure with extensive verandas on two street fronts.

Returning to its original name, The Waimate closed in 2018 for extensive renovations, reopening in late 2019. While retaining its handsome exterior (apart from the upper verandas), the interior underwent a radical change. The rabbit warren of small pokey rooms has been transformed into a single open space with a mezzanine floor; modern, airy and full of light, while the exposed brickwork and the old coal range from the original kitchen provides a cosy link to the past. Adding to the appeal is the extensive outdoor seating.

The menu is contemporary and modern, including innovative vegan and vegetarian dishes. Better still there is no chance to get bored with the food as the menu changes every six weeks. Another link to the past is the local beer, Toomey's Ale, brewed for the hotel in Christchurch using pure Waimate water.

MAKIKIHI COUNTRY HOTEL

36 Main South Road, (SH 1) Makikihi
Ph: 03 689 5709
Web: www.makikihihotel.co.nz
Food: Good country meals, with a reputation for excellent steaks.
Accommodation: Excellent rooms, clean, stylish and comfortable, with shared facilities. Seven rooms inside and four cabins outside.

Like so many old hotels, fire claimed the original two-storey Makikihi Hotel, which stood on the other side of SH1. Constructed to service the railway line, this was also the coaching stop where the horses were changed, so the hotel had to provide grazing, stables and a blacksmith in addition to accommodation and food. Rebuilt of double brick in 1929, the hotel went into a steep decline in recent years until the current owner, Bruce Milne, undertook extensive restoration in 2011.

Retaining many of the best original features, such as the wood panelling in the foyer and the main bar, the interior was carefully modernised so that today the Makikihi can claim to be a great, classic Kiwi pub.

The handsome main bar facing the main road still has the original fireplace, plus a wood burner to warm up the coldest South Canterbury night. Old wooden pews from the local St Mary's Church add to the warm atmosphere. On the wall are photos of the local rugby and netball teams, sponsored by the hotel. Beyond the bar is a separate pool room, and from there the hotel opens up to a wooden deck and an attractive garden bar centred on a fine old spreading elm, the ideal spot on a hot summer afternoon. Once a common feature in older hotels, the Makikihi retains the men's toilet outside by the entrance to the bar. Just quite why the men's toilets were outside remains a mystery.

WAIHAO FORKS HOTEL

4 Stoney Creek Road, (SH82) Waihao Forks
Ph: 03 689 2814
Built: 1913
Food: A wide variety of bistro meals including venison, salmon, steak and lamb, plus lighter meals and takeaways – you won't go hungry here.
Accommodation: Three hotel rooms with shared facilities, and a hunter's hut – prices negotiable based on amount of alcohol consumed.

La Tour Mollet d'Auvergne, better known as Ted, grew up and farmed in Waihao Forks, 10km south of Waimate. He enlisted in the New Zealand army on 19 September 1939 (his family were originally from Jersey in the Channel Islands, hence the unusual French name). As part of the 27th Machine Gun and Infantry Battalion, Ted was due to leave for overseas on 27 December 1939. After spending some time with his family he decided on a few beers at this local pub, the Waihao Forks Hotel, before the train left for Waimate and then on to Burnham Camp near Christchurch. Stories vary somewhat, but the most popular version is that Ted had lined up two bottles of his favourite brew, Ballins XXXX ale, but after finishing the first, the train whistle blew and Ted left the second bottle with publican George Provan to keep on the shelf for when he came home. Other versions of the story have Ted drinking in the pub as few days earlier and leaving the extra bottle with the publican, as the train he caught to Waimate would have left just after 7 am in the morning and it was unlikely that the pub would have been open at this time. Whatever the story, Ted never returned for his second bottle, because he died in battle among the vineyards of Crete on 2 June 1941, aged 35. However, in 1947 Ted's father received a letter from Yakovos Kalionzakis, a 17-year-old Cretan partisan, who found Ted wounded by a shot in the chest in the vineyard. Unable to move the badly wounded Ted, Yakovos managed to hide him from the Germans and brought him food for two days before Ted died. The family tragedy doesn't end there, as Ted's sister served in London during the war, driving fire engines, and she died there in 1945.

Today Ted's bottle is now an official RSA war memorial and each Anzac Day locals gather at the pub to pay their respects.

Bright and clean, this typically rural pub has rustic wooden tables down the centre of the room, all stamped with the brand marks of a local sheep farm. Just 10km south of Waimate on the road to Kurow, it would be disrespectful not to stop and have a beer to ensure that Ted and other men and women who never returned are not forgotten.

DUNEDIN & OTAGO

NORTH OTAGO

KUROW HOTEL

55 Bledisloe Street, Kurow
Ph: 03 436 0850
e: kurowhotel@gmail.com
Built: 1880
Heritage category 2
Food: Pub meals, with steaks and blue cod a speciality.
Accommodation: 16 upstairs rooms, some with en suites and the others
with shared facilities. Has a secure lock up for motorbikes and cycles.

Solidly constructed of local limestone by Mr B. Delargy in 1880, a year before the railway line reached Kurow, this was the second hotel in the township; the license was purchased and transferred from the Western Hotel, located near the river, which then closed down (the building still survives). During a particularly puritanical period, the local authorities banned music and dancing on licensed premises. However, the publican of the Kurow was undaunted and built a dance hall right next to the hotel (but not joined), so patrons could drink in the bar but still listen to music and dance. Now part of the main hotel, the hall is used for weddings and private functions.

Like the neighbouring Waitaki Hotel, the colours of the Kurow Hotel are unmistakeable, with the eastern half of the hotel in Speights colours and the western half in Dominion Brewery colours. They are a loyal lot in Kurow; the pub is also very proud of its All Black Captain Richie McCaw collection – Richie hails from the Hakataramea Valley on the other side of the river. Retaining old rimu and oak panelling, the hotel also retains separate public and lounge bars, and beyond that a sheltered sunny garden bar, just the spot in an area known for strong winds. In the lounge bar one wall is dedicated as the local RSA War Memorial.

WOWSER

The word 'wowser' was first used in the Australian publication the *Truth* in 1899, and originally meant a loud and disruptive person. Gradually during the early years of the twentieth century it both evolved in meaning and travelled to New Zealand, and came to mean someone of a puritanical nature who disapproves of alcohol, particularly in association with high spirits. It is usually used in a derogatory fashion. The origin of the word is unclear, though John Norton, editor of the *Truth* when the word was first used, claimed that it stood for 'We Only Want Social Evils Remedied'.

WAITAKI HOTEL

37 Bledisloe Street, Kurow
Ph: 03 436 0650
Built: 1940
Food: Pub meals, lighter fare and bar snacks.
Accommodation: 10 rooms with shared facilities.

In 1881 the branch line from Oamaru finally reached Kurow, 60km distant, and a few years later it crossed the Waitaki River to Hakataramea. As usual, a pub, known as the Bridge Hotel, sprang up just 50 metres from the station and, as usual, this hotel was destroyed by fire in 1907. Replaced by a new hotel, now known as the Railway Hotel, this also burnt down in the late 1930s. Single storey and constructed from stone, the replacement hotel opened in 1940, now facing the main road (Bledisloe Street). It was christened the Waitaki Hotel. Still standing, the hotel has been extended and is now double the size of the building erected in 1940.

Painted in bright colours, a single large bar/dining area runs across the front of the building, with the addition of outdoor seating in the front. A cosy hotel complete with log burner and historic photos, to the side of the pub is a small side window that serves as the drive through, making this possibly New Zealand's smallest bottle store.

BRYDONE HOTEL

115 Thames Street, Oamaru
Ph: 03 433 0480
Web: www.brydonehotel.co.nz
Built: 1881
Heritage category 2
Food: A very good a la carte restaurant.
Accommodation: 49 modern rooms, all en suite, 15 in the historic section of the hotel.

Starting life in 1874 as the Queen's Hotel, this simple wooden hotel burnt down in January 1880 with the loss of one life. James Markham, the owner, drew up plans for a much larger hotel and the new building, constructed of Oamaru stone, dominated the corner site on Thames Street, boasting 42 bedrooms, five family apartments, four sitting rooms, several bars and gas lighting. Despite the hotel's grandness, a police report in

1887 complained the hotel was 'badly conducted', with a reputation for drunkenness and fighting.

All that came to an end in 1905 when Oamaru voted to go dry and the hotel became the Queen's Private Hotel, though at one stage charges were laid against the publican for sly grogging. It was not until 1962 that Oamaru went 'wet' and was purchased by the local licensing trust. The hotel then changed its name to the Brydone Hotel.

Although much altered, with a modern extension added in 1975, the hotel still has considerable charm and architectural presence, making a significant contribution to Oamaru's heritage streetscape. Directly across the road is the grand Oamaru Opera house. The fine exterior of old Queen's Hotel is complemented by a tastefully decorated interior that is both traditional and modern. Outstanding features are the elegant curved staircase, the polished wooden floors and some of the original highly ornate plasterwork.

The main bar on the corner is friendly, comfortable and provides good service, while the adjoining dining room is grand and perfect for a special night out.

WET AND DRY

With the temperance movement gaining political influence, the government in 1893 allowed individual electorates to decide whether their area was to go 'dry'; that is, ban the sale of alcohol, or stay 'wet' – continue the sale of alcohol. The vote needed a two thirds majority and, no doubt influenced by the strong Presbyterian presence in the south and the fact that women could now vote, Clutha was the first electorate to go dry in 1894. A raft of other electorates followed in 1902, 1905 and 1908, and with them hotel closures in each of the areas that went dry. The first area to go back to being 'wet' was Ohinemuri (Coromandel), where the miners at Waikino were quick to replace the previous hotel that was pulled down. The result today is that in many areas of the country the old hotels have long disappeared. In a rare reversal, the Criterion Hotel in Oamaru closed when that area went 'dry' in 1906, and only reopened in 1998. Likewise, the Railway Hotel in Invercargill closed in 1906, and remained closed for over 60 years. Today it is one of Invercargill's finest historic buildings.

CRITERION HOTEL

3 Tyne Street, Oamaru
Ph: 03 434 6247
Built: 1877
Heritage category 1
Food: Better than average pub meals, with an emphasis on local specialities such as Aoraki salmon, lamb and Whitestone cheese.
Accommodation: Eight Edwardian style rooms with shared facilities.

Constructed of Oamaru stone from the Cave Valley quarries, the Criterion Hotel was built in the elaborate Victorian Italianate style and was designed by local architects Thomas Forrester and John Lemon for the hotelier William Gillespie. The upper floor of the hotel extended over the adjoining building, then a wool store and offices.

The good times were not to last and in 1905, after Oamaru went dry, the Criterion first ran as a temperance hotel and later as a boarding house, finally closing around 1940. Stripped of its ornamentation, the old hotel became a warehouse and a retail store, and by the 1980s was a mere shadow of its glorious past. Registered as a Category 1 historic place in 1987, the old pub was purchased by the Oamaru Whitestone Civic Trust, who set about restoring the building. It finally reopened as a hotel in 1998.

Today the Criterion is a popular destination for those soaking up the atmosphere of 'old Oamaru'. The small front bar is a busy, friendly place and reflects the size and ambience of a Victorian hotel while the polished floors, a fine wooden bar, historic photos and carefully chosen fittings combine to recreate the elegance of a bygone era. The original 'Ladies Bar' has been restored as The Snug, with a portrait of Ena Sharples presiding over the patrons, along with a Gentlemen's Smoking Room - minus the smoke.

DUNBACK INN

1200 Palmerston-Dunback Road, Dunback
Ph: 03 976 1589
e: dunback@xtra.co.nz
Built: 1864
Food: Bar snacks and full meals available on request.
Accommodation: Clean and comfortable rooms
ranging from shared facilities to en suite.

Built by Mr Parkhill, who laid the foundation in 1862, the Dunback Hotel opened for business in 1864 and is constructed from local schist and limestone, both of which are very abundant in the region. Formerly known as the Junction Hotel, it is located at the junction to Macraes Flat, the Northern Goldfields and the 'Pigroot' leading to the

Dunstan goldfields. On the main road just east of Dunback is Bowker Bridge, the last remaining stone bridge on the old coaching road to the Central Otago goldfields.

An important coaching stop, up to 100 wagons passed by each week as the township serviced miners on the way to the goldfields in the interior. As well as providing for passing trade, the hotel provided lodging for workers at the local rabbit canning factory and the lime works. The railway line ran right behind the hotel and Dunback was also the last stop for the train that carried limestone through to Dunedin. When the area voted to go dry in the early twentieth century, the hotel had a colourful reputation for sly grogging.

In 2007 the hotel was extended to create an attractive bar area, which opened out to the front of the hotel and out the back to an attractive garden bar, though today this handsome gold-era hotel is in need of a good tidy up.

STANLEY'S HOTEL

1760 Macraes Road, Macraes
Phone: 03 465 2400
e: stanleyshotel@xtra.co.nz
Built: 1882
Food: A la carte menu as well as bar meals.
Accommodation: Five comfortable rooms with shared
facilities and a self-contained studio.

Thomas Stanley, a proprietor of Macraes Hotel, employed a stonemason by the name of Budge to build his new hotel, which he naturally named Stanley's Hotel. Payment for the hotel was reputed to have been in beer and, although it is not recorded how much this was, local legend has it that Budge was paid two gallons per day of construction carried out. It was built in two sections, which allowed Stanley to commence trading while the second portion was still being built. Given the method of payment, it is no surprise that the hotel took five years to build, nor it is known what happened to the builder, but drinking two gallons of beer per day can't have made for a long and healthy life. Constructed of small blocks of local schist stone, a single large stone forms the lintels above the narrow windows and doors. The hotel still has two front doors side by side, one for the bar and the other for accommodation, as this allowed respectable women to enter the hotel without going through the bar.

When Stanley died in 1921 he transferred the ownership to his four daughters and not his son, George. The law prevented women from holding a liquor license, so George ended up as the licensee, but he took little part in running the business.

Gold mining is still a big industry in Macraes today and a mining company now owns the hotel, but it is privately run. Little has changed on the outside since the hotel was built, and across the road the hotel's original stables still stand. Inside the hotel has been spruced up to reflect the golden era of the late 1800s, with a cosy open fire and a warm local welcome.

WOMEN AND PUBS

Pubs were not the place for respectable women. Barmaids were banned from 1910 to 1961, and many pubs had a separate 'ladies bar' that could only be accessed from the street and had no internal connection to the main bar. Hotels were also notorious as dance halls and brothels, and local authorities tried to stamp out these activities. At Kurow Hotel when music and dancing was banned at licensed premises, the publican built a separate hall behind the pub for dancing and concerts in order to continue to attract patronage. An extraordinary photo taken of the Wakefield Hotel in the late nineteenth century shows a bare breasted woman at an upper-storey window, clearly displaying her assets. During the gold rush era, dancing girls were in high demand in goldfield hotels, and were lured across the Tasman by offers of high wages and payment of passage from Australia. The hours were demanding; a dancing girl was expected to work from 9pm to 6am.

DUNEDIN

CAREY'S BAY HISTORIC HOTEL

17 Macandrew Road, Carey's Bay, Port Chalmers
Ph: 03 472 8022
Web: www.careysbayhotel.co.nz
Built: 1874
Food: Given its location, it is not surprising that the hotel specialises in excellent dishes using fresh seafood sourced directly from the local fishing fleet.

The upper harbour at Dunedin is too shallow and the channel to narrow for anything other than small vessels, and from the beginning of European settlement in 1844 Port Chalmers was developed as the port for the city, making it New Zealand's third oldest town. Like Dunedin it has many fine stone buildings, most erected between1874 and 1880, and while these include churches and banks, as is fitting for a port town there are several great old pubs, including Carey's Bay Hotel (1874), Chicks Hotel (1876, now closed) and Port Chalmers Hotel (1875).

Known as the Crescent Family Hotel for more than 100 years, the hotel is constructed from local blue stone (volcanic breccia) and was in 1874 a state-of-the-art hostelry boasting 24 rooms with 'hot and cold, fresh and salt water baths'.

Just a short distance outside Port Chalmers, the hotel, then as now, overlooked the local fishing fleet and boatbuilders yards. When purchased by the late Cushla Martini and her husband, Barry Coleman, in 2001, the hotel was in very poor condition. Together they returned the hotel to its former glory before Cushla's death in 2005.

Stepping into the hotel today is like stepping back into the nineteenth century (and the very best of the nineteenth century). Warm wood panelling, original sash windows, a timber staircase and beautiful stone work over 140 years old together create one of New Zealand's best pub experiences. But the hotel is not all about history. The Carey's Bay Hotel also has an impressive collection of Ralph Hotere paintings, without doubt one of New Zealand's leading contemporary artists. Dining in the Conservatory is a treat and well worth the short drive out from Dunedin.

THE BOG/ROYAL ALBERT HOTEL

387 George Street, Dunedin
Ph: 03 477 8035
Web: www.thebog.co.nz
Built: 1864/1939
Food: The food has an Irish theme, though it is unlikely to be that Irish.

Occupying a hillside corner site, this striking hotel was originally built in 1864 as a single-storey wooden building called the Black Bull Hotel. In 1880, the new owner Daniel White rebuilt the hotel using the designs of local Italian architect Louis Boldini, who had drawn up the plans for the previous owner. Boldini was a prolific Dunedin architect, but most of his buildings have been demolished and the Royal Albert is his most significant remaining commission. White also changed the name to the Royal Albert Hotel. The enlarged hotel had a bar, three sitting rooms and a dining room on the ground floor, with the bedrooms and yet another sitting room upstairs. Two years later White lost his license on the grounds of 'immorality', having fathered several children to maids working in the hotel.

Under the ownership of Harry Allan, in 1939 the hotel was transformed by architects Stone and Sturmer from a Victorian hotel to a smart art deco building. Unlike the stark art moderne style fashionable in the 1930s, the Royal Albert is unique in being highly decorated, more in keeping with art deco styles from the late 1920s.

Close to the university, the Royal Albert was popular student pub, becoming a tavern in 1978. Later, in 1988, it was renamed the Albert Arms and given a Scottish theme. Today the old hotel, under the name the Bog, is now an Irish bar and confined single large bar and dining area on the ground floor. Friendly and relaxed, the Bog is fitted out with the usual faux Irish decoration and still attracts students and visitors drawn in by its stylish exterior.

DRINKING AGE

In 1970 the legal drinking age was reduced from 21 to 20, and in 1999, amid much debate, the age was lowered again from 20 to 18, though young people under this age can drink if alcohol is given to them by a parent or legal guardian. This does not include grandparents, aunts and uncles or older brothers and sisters. In 2006 a bill introduced to Parliament to move the age back to 20 was defeated.

THE KENSINGTON

4 King Edward Street, Dunedin
Phone: 03 455 8001
Web: www.thekensington.co.nz
Built: 1915
Food: Very pleasant dining area with all the pub meal favourites including an all-day breakfast, bar snacks, platters and separate lunch and dinner menus

Situated between the central city and South Dunedin, Kensington was once a bustling industrial suburb along the main road south with a residential area on the nearby slopes. Sport was pivotal as just to the south was the famous Carisbrook Park, while to the north was the huge Southern Recreation Ground, now known as The Oval.

At the heart of this busy area was the Kensington Hotel. Built in 1915, the hotel serviced the staunchly working-class suburb, but the twentieth century was not kind to this area and as the industry declined so did the Kensington.

Fortunately for the old hotel all was not lost as a change in ownership breathed desperately needed new life into the Kensington. Retaining some of the best features of the old hotel such as fine wooden floors, exposed brickwork, the original windows and grand staircase, the Kensington has been thoroughly modernised, but in a particularly good way. Gone are the pokey old bars and today the pub is spacious, light and stylish, and successfully combines a lively sports bar with the friendly atmosphere of the local pub.

THE LAW COURTS HOTEL

Corner of Cumberland and Stuart Streets, Dunedin
Ph: 03 477 8036
Web: www.lawcourtshotel.co.nz
Built: 1863/1937
Heritage category 2
Food: Wig 'n Pen Restaurant offering lunchtime roasts
and a selection of delicious evening meals.
Accommodation: Twenty-seven en suite rooms plus a three-bedroom
apartment. Established in 1863, it was original called the Auld Scotland
Hotel, but the name changed in 1902 to the Law Courts Hotel to reflect its
proximity to the grand and important Law Courts Building right next door.
Partially demolished and substantially rebuilt in 1937, the hotel morphed from
a three-storey Victorian building into a stylish four-storey art deco hotel.

Considered one of the most sophisticated and modern hotels in the country, the Law Courts Hotel was again refurbished for the visit of Queen Elizabeth and Prince Philip in 1954. The royal couple's suite was composed of a bedroom and lounge locally designed for the occasion, and contained Dunedin-made furniture. More importantly, the suite had a balcony, where the couple waved to a street packed with thousands of royalist fans.

In 1977 New Zealand Breweries purchased the building and made it part of their nationwide group, and again the interior was completely renovated; with the addition a Cobb and Co restaurant, now long gone.

Today the interior still retains many of the 1930s features, such as the stained wooden wall panelling, the open fireplace in the restaurant and the original staircase. Decorated throughout with old jugs, porcelain figurines and other memorabilia, the Wig 'n Pen Bar on the corner is named in honour of the local court system and features caricatures of judges and lawyers. The Law Courts is justifiably one of Dunedin's most popular hotels with visitors.

LEVIATHAN HOTEL

27 Queens Garden, Dunedin
Ph: 03 477 3160
Web: www.dunedinhotel.co.nz
e: leviathan@xtra.co.nz
Built: 1884
Food: Licensed restaurant offering a la carte meals in the evenings.
Accommodation: Seventy-seven rooms, all with en suites.

The name Leviathan comes from the Bible and is used to describe a huge creature, usually from the sea. In 1884 the Leviathan Railway Temperance Hotel was built, on land reclaimed from the harbour from rock dumped during the flattening of Bell Hill. Situated halfway between the city centre at the Exchange and the railway station and harbour, it was the ideal location for anyone visiting the city. It had 150 rooms and was reputed to be Australasia's largest hotel. In the 1950s the hotel was extensively modernised and, with en suites added, the number of rooms was cut in half. The Leviathan stayed a temperance hotel until it finally became licensed in 1974.

Many of the staff have witnessed a ghost on the third floor, believe to be Mrs Anstiss Silk, who ran the Leviathan from 1889 until her death in the hotel in 1899. Mrs Silk was a tough boss who insisted on very high standards of dress and behaviour from all her staff, and today the shade of Mrs Silk is keeping an eye on her hotel.

Located on a corner site, not far from the railway station, the Leviathan is indeed a large hotel. Shorn of its Victorian embellishments, the exterior is rather plain, but the inside is a delight. Although renovated over the years, many of the lovely stained-glass windows remain and the main dining room is fabulous, with a highly ornate plaster ceilings and elaborate archways. A grand staircase leads to the upstairs rooms. Just inside the main entrance are two magnificent marble statues of a lion and lioness, rescued from a Christchurch house destroyed in the earthquake, the largest of which weighs 500kg. What is not obvious from the outside is that the triangular building has at its heart a hidden courtyard where the horses were kept, and where the old stables still remain. This secret garden is just off the main bar.

TEMPERANCE HOTELS

Many of the early hotels did not serve alcohol and primarily provided accommodation and food for travellers. In the nineteenth century the line between hotels and boarding houses was very blurred, but boarding houses mainly catered for permanent residents and did not have a license to serve alcohol. These temperance hotels serviced a far more 'respectable' clientele than hotels, particularly for women, and specifically for women travelling unaccompanied by a man. Some city temperance hotels were set up to house the poor and assist them in avoiding the evils of drink, gambling and 'dissolute living'.

THE FABLE HOTEL

310 Princes Street, Dunedin
Ph: 03 477 1145
Web: www.fablehotelsandresorts.com
Built: 1879
Heritage category 1
Food: The Relish Bar and Restaurant serves a wide range of contemporary dishes.
Accommodation: Forty-eight boutique rooms, all with en suites.

The Moir Family Hotel was first opened on Manse Street in July 1862, but just two years later Andrew Moir sold the hotel to Job Wain, who already had substantial property interests in central Dunedin. Renamed Wains Hotel, the new owner quickly realised that the building was in the heart of the business district centred on the Exchange. Sensing an opportunity, in 1879 Wain had the hotel rebuilt at the extraordinary cost of 14,000 pounds. It was designed in the ornate Italianate Classical Renaissance style by local architects Mason, Wales and Stevenson. The finest materials were used: Oamaru stone for the walls, Otago breccia for the pediments, triple brick for the load bearing walls, and a slate roof. This magnificent exterior is still largely original.

Particularly impressive are the sculptures that run across the front of the hotel, which are said to be the handiwork of a master carver brought to New Zealand by William Larnoch to work on his castle out on the peninsula. The carvings represent Neptune and his offspring, and between these creatures is a crest of Prince of Wales feathers inscribed with 'Qui Va La' (who goes there).

Reputed to be one of New Zealand's most haunted buildings, the hotel has several ghosts, including a man dressed in 1940/50s clothing, said to be a former manager, and the shade of a Victorian woman. Children have been heard on the upper floors when no children were staying there.

Now known as The Fable Hotel, the interior is thoroughly modern, though the building still retains some features of the old hotel especially the fine plaster columns and cornices in reception and the lovely wooden staircase.

THE ROPE AND TWINE

Corner Macandrew Road and King Edward Street, South Dunedin, Dunedin
Ph: 03 455 2802
Built: 1875
Food: Excellent range of pub meals. The lunch time specials are a hot favourite.

In July 1875 when Nicolas Maloney opened his Ocean View Hotel in Forbury, South Dunedin, he was not shy about advertising his new establishment. The advertisement in the *New Zealand Tablet* read:

> *OCEAN VIEW HOTEL*
> *The above Hotel is one of the handsomest buildings around Dunedin, is situated within short distance of the Racecourse, and in close proximity to the Ocean Beach. It is built of concrete, is three storeys, and commands splendid views of Dunedin Harbour and the Peninsula, with Larnach's Castle in the distance. It will be fitted up with all the latest appliances, no expense being spared to make it one of the most comfortable homes in Otago. Travellers and others from the country will find it to their interest to inquire for the above Hotel. All wines and spirits of the best quality. Charges moderate, good stabling.*

Nicholas Maloney didn't stop there. In another advertisement he claimed that the Ocean View Hotel was the first concrete building of two floors, with the ground floor housing a bar and three palours, and a very handsome staircase leading to the upper floor, where there were two large sitting rooms and seven 'commodious' bedrooms. The top floor consisted of a balcony, while the hotel stable and other outbuildings occupied a quarter acre of land.

With that sort of confidence, it isn't surprising that Maloney was the first elected mayor of South Dunedin.

Recently renamed the Rope and Twine, this old South Dunedin hotel is today a gem in its own right. Retaining much of its Victorian exterior, the ambience inside the hotel is lovely. Many features such as the wood panelling, leadlight windows and old fireplace still remain. However, more importantly, the cosy style is matched by a warm and friendly atmosphere, making this a very popular local pub and a welcoming place for visitors.

THE PORTOBELLO HOTEL

2 Harington Point Road, Portobello, Dunedin
Phone: 03 478 0759
Web: www.portobellohotelandbistro.co.nz
Built: 1874
Food: A cut well above the average pub food.

A hotel existed in Portobello as early as 1867, but the hotel standing today began as a low, single-storey building in 1874, and was originally known as 'Coney's Hotel at Portbello'. To provide for ever increasing day-trippers from Dunedin, the hotel went up a storey at the beginning of the twentieth century, and a further low extension was added in 1908. Around 1912 the name changed to the Portobello Hotel.

Changing very little over the years, the hotel did escape the usual fate of old hotels – fire – but did not avoid a coat of stucco, frequently applied to give old buildings a more modern look and to make them more fire proof.

An attractive blend of historic and contemporary, the Portobello is the perfect halfway stopping point on a trip around the Otago Peninsula. Huge windows overlook the water, and the lovely outdoor area off the dining room is perfect on a sunny day. Along with local beers, the hotel has an excellent wine list, with most wines available by the glass. Featured in paintings by Robin White and Bill MacCormick, the hotel is popular with locals and visitors alike for its relaxed, charming and unpretentious atmosphere.

CENTRAL
OTAGO

DANSEYS PASS COACH INN

3476 Danseys Pass Road
Ph: 03 448 9048
Web: www.danseyspass.co.nz
Built: 1862
Food: Full a la carte menu with lighter snacks and coffee.
Accommodation: Fifteen rooms, seven en suite and eight shared facilities.

Edwin George built a simple wooden pub in 1860 to service coaches and miners crossing the difficult Danseys Pass on their way to goldfields further south. However, gold was discovered at nearby Kyeburn in 1862 and George decided to rebuild his inn of stone and earth, contracting a stone mason best known as Happy Bill. No doubt the 'happy' part of his name came from the unusual deal struck with Edwin: that for every schist boulder shaped and laid, Bill was to be paid one pint of beer. There is no record of how long it took to build the pub, but that it is still standing over 150 years later is testament to Happy Bill's skills, drunk or sober.

Typical of the multiple functions of a local hotel, in 1893 the hotel was used to hold both the inquest and the funeral services of three men, who were killed in an avalanche on the south face of Mount Nobbler as they attempted to rescue a local, Thomas Meikle, who later died of exposure.

One of New Zealand's iconic country hotel's, it is still a welcome sight for those travelling along the wild and dusty Danseys Pass Road, which, although much improved in recent years, is a challenging drive. For those not keen on the pass road, the road from Ranfurly and Naseby to the south is a good deal more relaxing.

Dansey's Pass Coach Inn has retained all the best features from the last 150 years, combining wood and local stone to create a warm and stylish interior. Originally the rooms would have been much smaller, but now they combine in one marvellous space, focusing on the large open fires that burn all winter.

A popular venue for conferences and weddings, the area boasts one of the highest sunshine hours in New Zealand, so this is also a great place to enjoy the garden bar or roadside tables. Whether you come over the pass from the north or up through the Maniototo, this pub is well worth the trip.

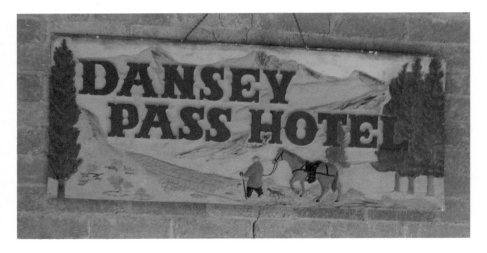

ROYAL HOTEL

1 Earne Street, Naseby
Ph: 03 444 9990
Web: www.royalhotel.co.nz
Built: 1863
Heritage category 2
Food: Good restaurant and café meals available.
Accommodation: Nine rooms, some with shared facilities and others with en suites.

Opened for business in October 1863, under the ownership of Andrew Morrison, the Royal Hotel no doubt attracted good custom by advertising that it had 'two young ladies available to dispense the miners their nobblers and change' (nobblers was slang for alcoholic drinks). Naseby became an important stop when Cobb and Co coaches began a service between Dunedin and Dunstan. Taking three days, the journey was broken in Naseby, where the horses were changed and the passengers given a break from the difficult and dusty journey. A dispute with the nearby Victoria Hotel over prices saw the Cobb's horses moved to the Royal Hotel stables in March 1870, though the extensive stables are long gone and have been replaced by a quiet beer garden.

When the railway was built between Dunedin and Middlemarch, Naseby became the halfway point of the shorter trip, but rather than just a stop, passengers travelling in either direction stayed the night at the Royal Hotel. Horses eventually made way to motorcars and by World War One the coaches were redundant.

The grand high façade disguising the long, low wooden building behind (later stuccoed) is typical of a modest goldfields hotels, most of which have now long gone. A lovely wooden terrace, open to the warm sunshine, has been added to the front of the hotel, making this the ideal spot for a quiet drink. Inside the large main bar/dining area, mining tools and old photos line the walls, keeping the gold mining days alive.

THE RANFURLY HOTEL

10 Charlemont Street, Ranfurly
Ph: 03 444 9140
Web: www.ranfurlyhotel.co.nz
Built: 1934
Food: Restaurant meals are available in the dining room and the bar.
Accommodation: Nineteen period rooms with both
en suite bathrooms and shared facilities.

By December 1897, the surveying of sections for the new township of Ranfurly had been completed, and the section on which the Ranfurly Hotel now stands was one of a number auctioned on 8 June 1898, and was bought by Peter Harrington for seventeen pounds and five shillings. Harrington, who owned the Commercial Hotel in Hyde, auctioned all that pub's chattels with the plan to transfer everything to a new hotel in Ranfurly. What happened to Mr Harrington's grand plan is not known, but on 1 November the property was leased to John Ryan, who went on to become the Ranfurly Hotel's first publican.

Fire swept through wooden Ranfurly Hotel in 1933, destroying the hotel along with the local hairdresser, the tobacconist shop and an unused building. Quickly rebuilt in the modern art deco style, the new hotel opened on 21 July 1934, and is believed to be the first hotel in New Zealand to comply with the new earthquake by-laws introduced after the Napier earthquake.

Little changed, the Ranfurly still maintains the stylish art deco theme outside, and inside in the reception, restaurant, bedrooms and lounge, with the original features enhanced by sympathetic redecoration. Not to be overwhelmed by history, the large public/sports bar out the back is as contemporary as any other pub.

WAIPIATA COUNTRY HOTEL

29 Main Street, Waipiata
Ph: 03 444 9470
Web: www.staywaipiata.co.nz
Built: 1932
Food: A blackboard menu that changes seasonally.
Accommodation: Six pleasant rooms, three en suite and three with shared facilities.

Four years after the Central Otago Railway Line reached town in 1895, the Waipiata Country Hotel opened for business. On Boxing Day 1932, while a town dance was in progress, a fire broke out in the hotel. The partygoers quickly became fire fighters. Using just buckets, they put out the fire, but not before it destroyed most of the two-storey building and claimed the life of boarder Jack Hayes. The fire left the mud brick part of the building intact (the black scorch marks are still there) and within ten short weeks a single-storey pub rose from the ashes. Recently discovered, the original blue prints for the reconstruction are now framed and hanging on the wall.

Long since closed, the old railway line is now part of the very popular Otago Central Rail, which opened in February 2000 and brought a new lease of life to the otherwise sleepy townships of the Maniototo Plain.

Well worth the ten minute drive from Ranfurly, the Waipiata Hotel has a spacious main bar and a separate dining area, along with a friendly atmosphere and a warm welcome. Carefully renovated, the owners have taken care to enhance the past but at the same time offer everything a modern traveller requires.

STRATH TAIERI HOTEL

25 Snow Ave, Middlemarch
Ph: 03 464 3288
Built: 1890s
Food: In summer, bistro meals plus blackboard specials are available
Monday to Sunday for early evening dining, and Friday, Saturday
and Sunday for lunch. In winter, evening meals only.
Accommodation: Seven comfortable rooms with shared
facilities, and undercover shelter for bikes.

Although no gold was discovered in the Strath Taieri valley, the town of Middlemarch developed to service the central Otago goldfields; first as a major stop for horse-drawn coaches and later as an important station when the railway reached the town in 1891. Built directly across the road from the railway station, the Strath Taieri Hotel is a short distance from the main road, State Highway 87. Today the hotel is a popular starting (or end) point for those cycling the Central Otago Rail Trail, and a popular destination for passengers on the historic Taieri Gorge railway line that runs regular train trips from Dunedin in the summer months.

With its distinctive western style frontage, the pub is the only one remaining of the town's original three hotels and, unusually for the period, it has never burnt down. The high façade hides a typical long, low building, with the stone front and a coat of stucco added much later. The side entrance to the hotel is flanked by two large limestone carvings depicting a merino ram and ewe. The interior has the very rustic feel of a typical Kiwi pub, and the hotel still runs its famous Singles Dance every two years at Easter, when bachelor farmers come looking for love.

THE VULCAN HOTEL

1670 Loop Road, St Bathans
Ph: 03 447 3629
Heritage category 1
Food: The Vulcan has a strong reputation for excellent homemade food and is open for breakfast, lunch and dinner.
Accommodation: Just four bedrooms with shared facilities – stay in Room One if you dare!!

Unlike the other mining towns of Central Otago, St Bathans, lying in the shadow of the Hawkdun Range and the Dunstan Mountains, flourished on both gold and coal mining. Gold was discovered here in 1863 and within short time a sizeable town sprang up, that at one stage boasted no fewer than 13 hotels. Mining for both gold and coal came to an end in 1934 and today very little remains of St Bathans, with the few surviving buildings strung out along a single main street. At the heart of the village is the legendary Vulcan Hotel. While most Central Otago hotels were constructed of stone, the single-storey Vulcan, built in 1882, is unusual in that it is made of dried mud bricks. Despite being a popular tourist attraction, the pub still retains a nineteenth century atmosphere, with a long low façade, narrow front bar and cosy dining room; all features typical of a small goldfield hotel.

The Vulcan has a notable ghost, but the jury is out on just who the ghost is and, more importantly, whether its intentions are benign or malevolent. Some say the ghost is that of a 'woman of the night', while other stories say she was a pregnant girl who was murdered, and yet another story has her as a jilted barmaid who drowned herself in the lake across the road. One version of the story is that the woman died in Room One, as it is in this room that most of the supernatural happenings occur. Some are mild, ranging from lights being turned off and on and feeling that someone else is in the room, through to ghostly specters and the feeling of being held down. During filming in the hotel, a television crew apparently encountered the ghost and were so frightened by the experience that they left immediately, with the filming incomplete. The pub hosts an annual 'Ghost To Ghost' Triathlon that starts and finishes under the window of Room One.

BECKS-WHITE HORSE HOTEL

4160 Becks-Lauder Road/SH 85, Becks
Ph: 03 447 3685
Web: www.beckshotel.co.nz
Built: 1864/1925
Heritage category 2
Food: Good country food, known for their steak and blue cod.
Accommodation: Two en suite rooms.

The tale of the White Horse Hotel is the story of two hotels. The original hotel was built of stone in 1864, by John Nixon Becks, as a rest stop for the coaching service along the Manuherikia Valley. This older part of the hotel displays an early example of recycling, as the foundations are made of empty beer bottles. An extension of wood and corrugation iron was added in 1884, and at that stage the hotel boasted ten rooms, two sitting rooms, a dining room that seated 16 people, stables and the local post office, to which was later added the telephone office. Interestingly, the hotel is located right on the 45 parallel, exactly equidistant from both the Equator and the South Pole, though whether this was intentional is not known.

In 1925 a new wooden hotel opened down the road, and over the years the old hotel has had a new life as a private home, and later as the general store. In recent years, local

folk have raised money to save this fine old hotel from deterioration, though at present only the exterior has been restored. The outbuildings have long since disappeared, though an ancient pear tree still survives in the dry Central Otago soil.

The 'new' pub has an attractive single bar and dining room, and is a particularly popular stop for those travelling the rail trail; the pub runs a courtesy van to the trail. More recently the owners of the hotel converted several front bedrooms into a successful antique store, which they later extended into the old hotel dining room. Known as the Glory Box Antiques and Collectibles, this is very likely the only licensed antique shop in the country.

OMAKAU COMMERCIAL HOTEL

1 Harvey Street, Omakau
Ph: 03 447 3715
Web: www.omakauhotel.co.nz
Built: 1898
Food: Good range of pub meals, including burgers and pizza,
matched by a good wine list with a focus on local vintages.
Accommodation: Ten rooms, en suite, plus a two-bedroomed cabin, a
bunkroom for backpackers and sites for caravans and campervans.

Constructed by William Leask in 1898 as a boarding house, in 1905 Leask obtained a license and changed the name to the Commercial Hotel, which he then owned for a further 20 years. Leask also farmed the land on which his boarding house was built, and the older schist stone stables, dating from around 1880, are now the hotel's function rooms. In 1921 Michael Perkins bought the hotel and extended the pub to twice the size, and this is the pub you see today. The Perkins family went on to own the hotel for the next 50 years.

Popular with locals and visitors, the heart of the pub is a combination bar and dining area that leads out to an attractive outdoor area, and at the centre of the bar is a robust log burner,, essential in the chilly winter months in Central Otago. Lining the walls are historic photos and memorabilia, that add to the old-world charm.

A separate dining room has the original dark oak panelling and the most extraordinary and extensive collection of miniature drink bottles, some of which are full while others are partly full or empty.

Adjoining the dining room is the Pomona Room, which is used as the breakfast room. Elegant, with original windows, wood panelling and an old open fireplace, the room also holds a large collection of water jugs, most branded by whiskey companies. The wood panelling extends into the reception area and the dining room.

In 2016 the Omakau Hotel won the Hospitality Industry Award for the Best Country Hotel, and it is not hard to see why.

BLACKS HOTEL

Corner Swindon Street and Ida Valley-Omakau Road, Ophir
Ph: 03 447 3826
Web: www.blackshotel.co.nz
Built: 1937
Food: Top of the range menu in the smart, recently extended dining room.
Accommodation: Ten stylish, themed rooms with en suites.

In contrast with the older pubs in Central Otago, the art deco Blacks Hotel built in 1937 appears incredibly modern. This is the third Blacks hotel in Ophir: the first wooden hotel built around 1870 burnt down, while the second stone hotel was left without customers when the road was realigned in the 1930s and bypassed Ophir completely. The town was once known as Blacks, after the Black brothers who discovered gold on their farm in 1863, and later changed to Ophir in 1875. Ophir was the legendary biblical land of the Queen of Sheba, who provided King Solomon with vast amounts of gold. The name of the hotel is the only remaining legacy from the earlier name.

Like several old hotels in this area, Blacks is a popular stop with those on the rail trail and it has been restored to enhance the art deco style. The exterior of the hotel is largely original, while inside the old ceiling and some of the wood wall paneling remains. The bar features a fabulous pair of sandblasted glass doors from the 1950s, part of a liquor company advertising campaign – one door features Johnnie Walker Whisky and the other door Beefeater Gin. On the wall is a wonderfully old photo of the hotel on the day it opened. In addition to the large bar and dining room, there is a great outdoor terrace, just the spot to put your feet up with a long cool beer after a hard day biking the rail trail.

CHATTO CREEK TAVERN

1544 Omakau-Chatto Creek Road/SH 85, Chatto Creek
Ph: 03 447 3710
Web: www.chattocreektavern.co.nz
Built: 1886
Food: The tavern is open for lunch and evening meals, and is well known for good hearty food and country cooking.
Accommodation: Although a tavern, Chatto Creek offers both backpacker and four double rooms with shared facilities.

The first hotel, known as the Three Horse Shoes, was established as a rest stop for both Cobb and Co coaches and bullock trains making their way up the Manuherikia Valley from Alexandra. Constructed of wood, this hotel burned down and was replaced in 1886 by a much more substantial (and fire proof) building of mud brick and stacked stone.

Chatto Creek in the late nineteenth century was a flourishing settlement of around 800, supported by the construction of the railway and as a depot for those employed by the rabbit board, as rabbits at this time were (and still are) a major pest in the district.

Today Chatto Creek has a more modest population of around 20, but it's a lively and busy stop for those on the Central Otago Rail Trail (Chatto Creek is usually the first stop on the trail). The tavern is everything a country pub should be. The main bar is dominated by a beautiful old stone fireplace, and it has a warm and welcoming country ambience. On the walls are several beautiful old guns, including a 350-year-old Afghani Galil gun and a 300-year-old gun that once belonged to a Belgian highwayman. A pleasant dining room is off the bar and behind the pub is a large shady garden bar, that backs right onto the rail trail and even provides hammocks for those particularly in need of resting their weary legs.

The pub is the home of the local Chatto Creek Curling Club and right next door is the Chatto Creek Post Office. Opened in 1892, this post office was originally a canvas tent a few metres square with just one window, and it claims the record as New Zealand's smallest post office. Later, the building had corrugated iron nailed over the canvas, though the original cloth material is still visible on a section of the inside wall. The pub narrowly escaped destruction in June 1990 when a freak wind storm lasting just eight minutes hit the tavern in the early hours of the morning. The roof was completely ripped off and pieces of iron were found up to eight kilometers away.

In 2013 the hotel won the Hospitality Association Awards as Best Country Hotel.

THE VICTORIA ARMS HOTEL

65 Melmore Terrace, Old Cromwell Town, Cromwell
Ph: 03 445 0607
e: vicarms2017@gmail.com
Built: 1863
Food: Bistro meals with a focus on traditional pub dishes.
Accommodation: Eight clean and tidy rooms with shared facilities.

In 1862 two miners discovered gold just downstream from the junction of the Clutha and Kawarau Rivers, and within a few months thousands of miners, traders and businesses descended on the area, all looking to make a fortune. Cromwell boomed but, as always, the gold ran out and slowly through the first half of the twentieth century the town declined. In 1965 the government announced the building of a hydro-electric dam at Clyde, just upriver from Alexandra, a project that would result in flooding the old town of Cromwell. In 1992 Lake Dunstan began to fill and in 1994 the Clyde Dam officially opened. Prior to the inundation, the most important of the heritage buildings were moved to higher ground, just above the waters of the new lake and right alongside the old Victoria Arms hotel.

Now the only old Cromwell pub on its original site, the Victoria Hotel was built in 1863, just one year after the initial discovery of gold, and it was one of nine hotels in the main street of Cromwell. When Cromwell was flooded only two remained. The first owner, Mrs A. Bell, had the hotel until 1877, when she sold to Mr James Stuart, who in turn owned the hotel until 1899. After his death, his wife continued to run the business and extensively altered the hotel around 1900. Typical of era, the low building was constructed of schist stone and timber.

Standing in the pub today trying to work out the layout of the original hotel is like solving a very tricky puzzle. Sections of old stone walls, doorways and a fine old fireplace have been incorporated into the huge main bar, which looks out over the waters of the lake just below. Originally known as the 'top' pub, the Victoria Hotel was renamed the Victoria Arms Hotel in the 1960s, and the former competitors, the middle and bottom pubs, are now deep under water. The modern restaurant extension has a huge outdoor terrace with views of the lake.

BANNOCKBURN HOTEL

420 Bannockburn Road, Bannockburn
Ph: 03 445 0615
Web: www.bannockburnhotel.com
Built: 1930s
Food: Open for lunch and dinner, the Bannockburn has a classy
pub style menu but with a emphasis on sharing meals and larger
platters, matched by the famous Central Otago wines.

Although Bannockburn has a long history as a gold mining down, the current Bannockburn Hotel is, by Central Otago standards, fairly new. The original settlement, established in 1862, was much lower down by the river, an area today that is under the waters of Lake Dunstan. The pub that existed in this village was moved to the area known as Doctor's Flat in 1877 (modern day Bannockburn). A simple timber building, it was later re-clad in corrugated iron and was just one of several hotels in the town. Eventually the hotel was demolished in the 1930s and rebuilt on the same site in the art deco style.

Today the single-storey stucco Bannockburn Hotel occupies a superb site, overlooking Cromwell town and in the distance the Pisa Ranges and Mount Difficulty. The hotel

has one main bar that has a spacious open feel, but at the same time retains a warm, friendly atmosphere, enhanced by the comfy couches spread in front of the open fire. The dining room takes advantage of the fantastic view, with indoor and outdoor dining, however if the wind is a bit blustery in front, out the back of the pub is a huge sheltered garden bar. Situated in the heart of Central Otago wine country (the first Central Otago vineyards were established around Bannockburn in 1992), the hotel features a wine list

with over 200 wines, and while the focus is on local wines, there is also a good offering of international labels. More than 80 wines are available by the glass, so it's just the place for a spot of local wine tasting.

The pub is the area's unofficial mountain bike headquarters and the famous, but grueling, Pub-to-Pub race starts at Garston and finishes at Bannockburn, while the Mountain Bike Classic starts and finishes at the Bannnockburn Hotel.

THE CARDRONA HOTEL

Cardrona Valley Road, Cardrona
Ph: 03 443 8153
Web: www.cardronahotel.co.nz
Built: 1863
Heritage category 2
Food: The Cardrona provides a good range, from light fare through to more substantial meals.
Accommodation: Fourteen modern en suite rooms in a cottage style annex in the traditional fashion, opening out through French doors to the hotel's cottage gardens.

The Cardrona Hotel is legendary, and claims that it is the most photographed hotel in New Zealand are not exaggerated. Almost an architectural style in its own right, the hotel, simple in style, is an excellent example of the small wooden hotels that blossomed virtually overnight to service the burgeoning population on the goldfields. Situated in the Cardrona Valley between Queenstown and Wanaka, the township in its heyday had at least four hotels. While the fortunes of the town have waned and the population has drifted away, the Cardrona Hotel survives, but only just.

Jim Patterson is without a doubt the hotel's most colourful publican. Jim initially worked a gold claim in the valley before taking over the hotel in 1926, and he ran the pub until his death in 1961 at the age of 91. Jim was eccentric to say the least. He refused to serve women and Jim, not the customer, decided how much they could drink. If you were travelling in the direction of Queenstown over the Crown Range, then one drink was the limit, but if you were going towards Wanaka then you could have two drinks. His signs strung out along the road were famous, and one still exists by the front door to the hotel: 'If you have a Shilling Stop, if not Step on it.' The old, narrow bar that Jim presided over is still in the hotel and his benign ghost is said to linger at the hotel. After Jim's death the hotel closed and was finally saved from dereliction, first reopening as a restaurant in 1983 and with accommodation added in 2002.

What makes the Cardrona so appealing is that while it has all the facilities of a modern hotel, it has successfully preserved the most attractive features of the historic pub. It is much bigger than the narrow wooden frontage suggests, but it manages to keep that warm friendly ambience that only an old building can impart. Behind the hotel the large garden is a real surprise. In summer the garden is shady and colourful with flowers, while in winter it is warmed by an outdoor fireplace and braziers.

Next door, the old school house has been developed into a gift shop, and outside the hotel is a vintage Chrysler that adds to the hotel's photogenic appeal.

LUGGATE HOTEL

60 Main Road, SH 6, Luggate
Ph: 03 443 8523
Built: 1881
Food: Not an extensive menu, but one that ticks all the "pub meal" boxes.

Typical of a goldfields' hotel, the Luggate began its life in 1867 as a simple wooden building known as the Albion Hotel to service the alluvial gold workings between Wanaka and Cromwell. Like many country hotels, the pub also owned land across the road to accommodate stock being driven to market and ran horse sales, all activities that guarantee to boost business.

In 1881 the new owner Thomas Trevathan replaced the old wooden hotel with the schist stone building that is still standing today. Originally, the hotel would have been a maze of tiny rooms, accommodating a main bar (all drinking was done standing up) as well as sitting rooms, one each for men and women, a dining room and of course tiny bedrooms that held a bed and not much else. Out the back were the stables and outhouses. In 1969 the hotel became the Luggate Tavern, though old name lives on in the local Luggate Albion Cricket Club.

The exterior is little altered since built 140 years ago, but the interior has changed radically. Today the hotel is simply two large areas, the main bar and a dining room, plainly decorated but comfortable enough. The backyard is now the popular garden bar. As the oldest pub in the area and the closest to the Wanaka airfield, this pub has a reputation for good hospitality with locals and visitors alike.

MILLERS FLAT TAVERN

5592 Ettrick-Raes Junction Road, Millers Flat
Ph: 03 446 6025
Web: www.millersflattavern.co.nz
Built: 1926
Food: Known for its blue cod and steak meal, the menu includes
lighter meals, blackboard specials, bar snacks and kid's options.
Accommodation: Two rooms with shared facilities. The
local camping ground is just over the river.

Little is known about the first Millers Flat hotel, which stood on the other side of the road by the river. Built of wood and two-storeyed, some time later the hotel lost its top floor and it was eventually replaced by a new hotel in 1926. The site for the new hotel, across the road and away from the river, was on land previously occupied by Campbell's Garage, the earliest building in the area and the coach stop for Cobb and Co. The builder, Tom Butler, was also responsible for the construction of the hotels at Beaumont and Raes Junction. While it is a credit to his building skills that all three hotels still stand today (Raes Junction is closed), Mr Butler's financial skills left a lot to be desired – he forgot to include the price of the bricks in his quote for this hotel.

In 1965 it was converted to a tavern and, more recently, it has undergone a much-needed renovation and now includes accommodation. The single bar/dining area is bright and sunny and decorated with historic photos, including many of local trucking companies. Without music or a pool table, the owners take pride in their place being a 'talking pub'. While there is a small deck just off the bar, the place to be on a hot, sunny summer's day is the 'garden bar'; a grassy area with outdoor seating under a huge, shady weeping willow, just off the car park.

THE BEAUMONT HOTEL

1897 State Highway 8, Beaumont
Ph: 03 485 9431
Web: www.beaumonthotel.co.nz
Built: 1938
Food: Good honest pub food, including great steaks and pizza as
well as coffee and bar snacks. A few dishes come with an Icelandic
twist (one of the owners is also the chef and is from Iceland).
Accommodation: Seven rooms with shared facilities and a camping ground
with power sites for tents and campervans (and cabins in the near future).

During the gold rush days of the 1860s, a township was surveyed on both sides of the Clutha River and became known as Beaumont. In 1863 dredging for gold in the river at Beaumont began, and by 1870 it was a bustling community with three hotels. The original Bridge Hotel, constructed in 1878, was a grand two-storey building with ornate verandas running around the entire building. Burnt down in 1931, it wasn't rebuilt until 1938, this time as the more modest single-storey brick building that stands today. Local builder Tom Butler clearly could turn his skills to most things, as not only did he build this hotel, but also the town bridge and two more hotels at Raes Junction and Millers Flat.

In the side porch is a curious pattern, which local legend has it was incorporated into

the building by a German working for Tom. However, what first appears to be a Nazi Swastika is an ancient symbol for good luck. In the Nazi version the swastika arms are on an angle, whereas in the sign for good luck the arms are upright.

Beyond the hotel, very little of the old township exists today. While the gold has long gone, farming, forestry and apple orchards flourish, and visitors can enjoy trout fishing, hunting and bush walks.

Family run and friendly, the Beaumont Hotel (and camping ground) is a treat. Hung with hunting trophies and old photos, the main bar runs across the front of the building, centred on a log burner for those damp, chillier winter days. The separate dining room has stunning plaster ceilings and a beautiful, tiled fireplace, and two more original fireplaces are in the bar – clearly Tom the builder had an eye for detail. If you are staying in the hotel, check out the beautiful wooden linen cupboards that line the passage.

SOUTHLAND

GARSTON HOTEL

8 Garston-Athol Hwy, Garston
Ph: 03 248 8989
Built: 1939
Food: Tasty pub meals, reasonably priced, plus a good
stop for a coffee, cake or a lighter snack.
Accommodation: Seven rooms, a mixture of en suite and
shared facilities, plus a bunkroom for backpackers.

Built in 1877 in anticipation of the new railway line to Kingston, and supplying miners at the nearby goldfields at Nokomai and Nevis, the first hotel at Garston was a long, low building constructed from local stone. Running from Invercargill to Kingston and grandly known as the Great Northern Railway, the railway reached Garston in 1878 and there pushed on to Kingston, just 20km away, where passengers and goods were loaded aboard steamers for the trip up the lake to Queenstown. This modest hotel was superseded in 1912 by a much larger two-storey wooden hotel, which, unsurprisingly, went up in flames in 1935. Finally replaced four years later by a more modest, single level building in the art deco style, the hotel today has changed very little from that time, apart from the bar extension in 1967. Part of the old hotel from Parawa has been moved behind the pub and is used as staff accommodation.

Currently being renovated, the current owners are tastefully combining the best of art deco style with modern facilities. To the left of the main entrance is a welcoming dining area, with polished wood floors and wooden furniture in keeping with the 1930s period. To the right is a friendly bar that is typical of many country pubs. Today trout fishing and cycling attracts the visitors to Garston, and the Around the Mountains Cycle Trail passes right by the pub.

NIGHTCAPS HOTEL

1 Clapps Street, Nightcaps
Ph: 03 225 7332
e: nightcapshotel@xtra.co.nz
Food: Pub meals, burgers and bar snacks – they know how to feed people here.
Accommodation: Nine rooms with shared facilities.

Nightcaps and nearby Ohai sit on a huge field of lignite, or brown coal, and from 1880 coalmining flourished, first in Nightcaps, and from the 1920s in Ohai. Like all coal towns in New Zealand, the population of both Ohai and Nightcaps has declined, and since 2003 opencast mining has replaced underground mining.

The Railway Hotel built in 1887 was a grand, two-storey affair, but, in an all-too-familiar tale, it burnt down in the 1940s. The replacement building, still standing today, was opened in 1948 in the classic art deco style of the 1930s. Very few changes have been made to the exterior, making this a very fine example of art deco architecture, which is also reflected in the nearby Town Hall that was built during the same period, after the old hall burnt down. An art deco hotel at Ohai (now closed) was also built around the same time, though this time fire played no part, as this was the first hotel to be built in that settlement. Fireproofed by massive concrete walls 12 inches thick, and reinforced with old iron railway tracks, this Railway Hotel is one pub that is built to last. In more recent years the name of pub was changed to Nightcaps Hotel.

Open and lit from the numerous windows across the front of the hotel, the main bar/dining area features tables and a bar top of beautiful polished wood. A log burner keeps the bar snug in winter. A strong union town, on one wall are several miner's hats bearing the names of their owners, that go back several generations and have long been a feature of the hotel.

MOSSBURN RAILWAY HOTEL

16 York Street, Mossburn
Ph: 03 248 6399
Web: www.mossburnhotel.co.nz
Built: 1923
Food: Pub meals that are a cut above the average and include
sharing platters, burgers, wraps pizzas and bar snacks.
Accommodation: Ten rooms, some en suite and some with
shared facilities. Across the road in a separate building that
used to be a diner are eight rooms, all with en suites.

With the expectation of the railway reaching Mossburn in 1885, George Beer moved his hotel from Castle Rock, near Lumsden, to Mossburn. Unfortunately for the aptly named Mr Beer, the depression of the 1880s delayed construction, and the although the line started in 1880, it didn't reach Mossburn until 21 January 1887. The line quickly provided access to the outside world and, along with the town, the pub flourished as the line ran next to the hotel (just to the right of today's pub). In addition, the hotel also owned the local stockyards.

Notable New Zealand poet Bill Manhire was born in Mossburn; the son of the publican, he grew up in the pub. He retains both fond memories and a strong connection to his childhood town and the pub has dedicated a wall to their most famous son.

When the old wooden hotel burnt down, the present hotel was opened, in May 1923, and this time it was constructed in brick. A second storey was added in 1935. However, the good times were not to last and when the passenger service was axed on 4 October 1937, Mossburn slowly declined.

The hotel was then mainly used to house contractors working in the area, but more recently tourism has boosted the fortunes of both the town and the hotel. Renovated in 1987 and again more recently, the lovely dining room evokes an earlier era and features historic photos on the wall, while the main bar opens onto a garden bar, centred on a beautiful old spreading elm.

This is one hotel worth the short detour off SH 94, near the junction with SH 97 (Queenstown to Te Anau).

CENTRAL SOUTHLAND LODGE

232 Great North Road, Winton
Ph: 03 236 8413
Built: 1911
Heritage category 2
Food: Bistro meals available Thursday to Sunday.
Accommodation: Nine upstairs rooms with shared facilities, offering a comfortable night's rest.

Pubs were frequently known in a town as Top, Middle and Bottom pub. This had nothing to do with quality, but merely reflected geography, the Top being at the north end of the town, the Bottom at the south, and the Middle is obvious. Winton is the only town in New Zealand where all three pubs still exist.

The grandest of these, 'the Middle Pub', opened in 1911 to replace the Railway Hotel that burnt down the year before, in a fire that destroyed several buildings in the town. The old Railway Hotel, built in 1861 to service the railway from Invercargill, was also a grand building, with 25 rooms and stables for 100 horses.

Designed in the Neo-Classical style by Invercargill architect C.J. Brodrick, the new Railway hotel dominated the small town of Winton and including several ground floor shops as well as accommodation, restaurant and bar. In 1993 the changed the name to the Central Southland Lodge.

Today the hotel is as much a community centre as a pub with the main bar on the corner and behind that the dining room and sports bar including a TAB. Everywhere in the hotel are framed photos both historical and of local sports teams sponsored by the pub including teams in the Tour of Southland, New Zealand's most famous cycle race.

OTAUTAU HOTEL

167 Main Street, Otautau
Ph: 03 225 8166
Web: www.otautauhotelpub.co.nz
Built: 1907
Food: Excellent pub menu including a classic mixed grill,
excellent salads, pizza and a kid's menu.
Accommodation: Five rooms with shared facilities, plus a self-contained studio.

Situated on the banks of the Aparima River and lying at the foot of the forest-covered Longwood Ranges, visitors usually bypass this very pretty Southland town and thereby miss one of the region's most attractive small pubs, the Otautau Hotel.

Constructed from timber in 1893, fire swept through the building in the early hours of Saturday 23 June 1907. The blaze started in a back bedroom, very likely caused by someone smoking in bed (the usual cause of hotel fires), and it quickly consumed the hotel, with one guest leaping out a window to escape. The conflagration, fanned by strong westerly winds, spread, destroying the National Bank and the local tailors and taking the life of hotel guest Mr W. Carnharn, who was in Otautau attending the horse sales. Fully insured, the hotel was rebuilt the same year, this time in fireproof brick.

Retaining its fine Edwardian exterior, the Otautau Hotel has immediate street presence in this small town, while inside a smart contemporary bar/dining area runs the full length of the hotel and beyond to a sheltered terrace. Serving great food, this is one of Southland's most appealing country hotels.

CARRIERS ARMS HOTEL

96 Palmerston Street, Riverton
Ph: 03 234 8506
Built: Early 1928
Food: Main menu has an emphasis on fresh fish, plus lighter meals and bar snacks.
Accommodation: Six comfortable rooms with shared facilities.

John Paulin and his wife Ann (the half sister of Captain John Howell, who ran the whaling station at Riverton from 1836) arrived in New Zealand in 1843 and set up home in Riverton. Later, in 1852, their home became the Eastbourne Hotel. Under publican John Vaughan, the hotel changed its name to the Carriers Arms in 1873.

An old photo on the pub wall shows the Carriers Arms as a substantial two-storey brick building, but this didn't prevent the hotel from burning down on Tuesday 29 October 1927. The fire started in the wooden kitchen at the rear of the hotel, and quickly spread to the heart of the hotel, taking the lives of Mrs William Trembath and her five-year-old daughter, Moira – the wife and daughter of the publican. With the insurance payout of 2,850 pounds, William Trembath rebuilt immediately and reopened in 1928, though this hotel was a modest, single-storey brick building. In 1930 he changed the name of the hotel to Trembath's Hotel, but later the name reverted to the Carriers Arms.

A friendly local pub in one of New Zealand's oldest towns, the single main bar runs along the front of the hotel and extends through a small dining area, then out to a sunny terrace.

COLAC BAY TAVERN

15 Colac Bay Road, Colac Bay
Ph: 03 234 8399
Web: www.colacbaytavern.co.nz
Built: 1938
Food: Good pubs meals, with fish and steak a speciality, as well as lighter meals, pizza and gourmet burgers.
Accommodation: Colac Bay Holiday Park is part of the pub complex and offers cabins, tent sites and camper van sites.

When the railway line reached Colac Bay in 1881, the long sweep of white sand beach became a popular destination for day trippers from Invercargill. Two modest hotels sprang up in 1882; one of these was the Railway Hotel, with Edward Hopgood as its publican. The itchy-footed Mr Hopgood drifted away the following year, leaving his industrious wife Susan in charge, who, in addition to the hotel, ran a grocery store and the post office. Later Susan's sons, Charles and William, also ran the hotel. By 1900 Colac Bay had three hotels, a post office and several shops, and a population of around 2,000.

The Railway Hotel burnt down in 1936, and the story is that the fire was able to take hold because the publican was totally engrossed listening to an All Black game on the radio. Replaced two years later by a modest building of stucco over brick, the railway continued to run right past the hotel (where the camping ground is today) until it closed in 1976. The beach at Colac Bay is famous for its excellent surf and the small settlement is a popular spot for those touring the southern coastline.

A large, sunny bar/dining area with a cosy log burner runs right across the front of the hotel and out onto a huge sheltered deck with a wood-fired pizza oven. Opening early to service the camping ground, the pub includes a small general store and serves meals from breakfast to dinner. The current owner also has a fishing boat and the blue cod on the menu is guaranteed to be the freshest you will find anywhere. The tavern is just a short walk to the beach.

THE WHITE HOUSE

22 Wallacetown-Lorneville Highway, Invercargill
Ph: 03 235 8116
Built: 1887
Food: Good hearty pub food – you won't go hungry.

Not the first pub on this site, the original Junction Hotel built in 1860 succumbed to fire in 1886, and its replacement lasted just one year before being again destroyed in 1887. Rebuilt yet again, this hotel still survives (possibly helped by a coat of stucco in 1926), though modern additions have all but swamped the old 1887 pub that still forms the heart of this famous hotel.

Nor was this the only pub on this busy intersection just north of Invercargill at Wallacetown. A short distance away was the rival pub, Wallacetown Hotel, and when the Junction Hotel changed its name to the Wallacetown Junction Hotel the Licensing Commission stepped in to sort out the confusion. In 1922 it was decided that the Wallacetown Hotel (still standing) was to be known as Green Roofs Hotel, and the Wallacetown Junction Hotel as the White House Hotel.

In 1905 the Invercargill and Mataura electorates voted by a narrow margin to go 'dry', while central and western Southland (including Bluff) stayed 'wet'. The White House hotel just north of the city became the nearest watering hotel for Invercargill drinkers, and immediately a horse-drawn tram service ran from the city to Lorne Corner and the White House. It was said that local taxis made more money from running alcohol into the city than from passengers.

The area, now known as Lorneville, not only attracted the city folk but also became the location of major stockyards (which are still behind the hotel) and a large freezing works later moved to Makarewa. The White House long remained the favourite stopping point for farmers heading home from a day out 'in town'.

While heady days of yesteryear are gone, recent changes have seen the huge main bar turned into a more modern style café and bar, including a small gift shop. One thing that hasn't changed is the toasty wood burning fire that has kept several generations of Southlanders warm in this classic pub.

THE GRAND

76 Dee Street, Invercargill
Ph: 03 928 5750
Web: www.thegrandinvercargill.co.nz
Heritage category 2
Accommodation: Fifty-seven rooms, all en suite.

Dating from the 1880s, the Prince of Wales Hotel originally stood on this site and was destroyed by fire. In its place rose the impressive Grand Hotel, opened in 1913, which quickly became the leading hotel in the city. The architect, Cuthbert John Brodrick, was born in Invercargill, attended Southland Boys High School and designed several major buildings in the city, as well as the Southland Lodge Hotel in Winton. Constructed after the city went dry, the Grand gained its reputation on excellent food, stylish function rooms and modern accommodation. Most famously, the hotel hosted the Queen and Prince Phillip on their tour of Southland in 1954.

Now just offering accommodation, the heritage building retains its impressive Edwardian exterior in the heart of Invercargill, though at street level it is rather ordinary. Restoration of the hotel is an ongoing process and far from complete. Several enormous reception rooms on the first floor are especially impressive, and although not in the best condition feature intricate plaster ceilings, massive ornate mirrors and period fireplaces. Holding pride of place in a corner lounge are the two chairs used by Queen Elizabeth and Prince Philip to make their final radio farewell to the people of New Zealand in January 1954.

VICTORIA RAILWAY HOTEL

3 Leven Street, Invercargill
Ph: 03 218 1281
Web: www.hotelinvercargill.co.nz
Built: 1896
Heritage category 1
Food: Gerrard's Restaurant provides a good selection of evening meals, some
made with local produce. Breakfast is also available for hotel guests only.
Accommodation: Eleven comfortable, refurbished rooms,
with en-suite bathrooms and all amenities.

Located opposite the railway line and former station, in the heyday of train travel the
Railway Hotel would welcome alighting travellers in droves. If the walls could talk…
The lounge bar and Gerrard's Restaurant ooze atmosphere and it's easy to imagine the
frivolities and merriment of a bygone era, in the height of the development of the Main
South Line and the ensuing popularity of train travel.

The original Smith's Railway Hotel, erected on the site in 1876, was constructed from
wood. In 1896, Mrs Watson commissioned a replacement hotel, and the imposing brick
building that stands today was built, together with stables. In 1906 the hotel was forced
to close due to the temperance movement and prohibition in Invercargill.

In 1967, the hotel was purchased by Keith and Margaret Gerrard and became known as Gerrard's Private Railway Hotel. The Gerrard family ran the hotel from 1967 to 2000. In 2003, it was closed for renovation.

Now known as the Victoria Railway Hotel, the hotel accommodates fewer guests than it did under Mrs Watson's ownership; parts of the original building had to be removed because it was on the neighbour's land. The dining room has high ceilings and blue pillars, evoking a sense of grandeur. Oil paintings, old photos and antique fixtures adorn

the walls. The bar is cosy, with a small servery and stained-glass window features. Only hotel guests can use the bar and restaurant though, due to license requirements.

The Victoria Railway Hotel is an architectural highlight, and is once again popular with corporate and leisure travellers, as well as railway enthusiasts who are perhaps less raucous than the guests of old.

EAGLE HOTEL

134 Gore St, Bluff
Ph: 03 212 8134
Built: 1953
Food: Excellent, innovative menu and a very good reason to stop here.
Accommodation: Ten rooms with shared facilities.

Not that long ago a number of old pubs lined the busy main road through the port town of Bluff, but today the Eagle Hotel is the last old pub standing. Dating back to 1870, an historic photo on the wall shows a fine wooden hotel, which was consumed by fire, as were two of its replacements. Razed completely in 1953 and rebuilt the same year, the building standing today is largely from that time, though the hotel was badly damaged yet again by fire in 1976.

Despite trial by flames, the hotel today is an attractive pub despite the rather plan frontage, and much of the interior reflects the 1950s style with a contemporary flair. With wooden floors and wall panelling, and old photos focusing on Bluff shipping lining the walls in both the front bar and the dining room, the hotel has a sense of history. Locals are very loyal to the Eagle, and if you are dropping by for an afternoon brew, take time to chat with well-known local Harp, the former owner and skipper of the boat *Daphne*.

SOUTH SEA HOTEL

26 Elgin Terrace, Oban, Stewart Island
Ph: 03 219 1059
Web: www.stewart-island.co.nz
Built: 1926
Food: Good pub grub, with an emphasis on local fish and seafood specials.
Accommodation: Hotel rooms above the pub, with shared facilities and a guest lounge. Separate motel-style units and a cottage at the rear of the premises.

Proclaiming itself a living monument to good times, the South Sea Hotel is a vibrant gathering place for locals and visitors, and is as much a museum of Stewart Island social

history as it is a watering hole. 'These wooden floors have squeaked under the feet of the famous and infamous,' one of the pub's signs explains.

Oban House was originally built on the site in 1890, next to a mill. In 1899 it was enlarged to almost double its original size, and a store was added by proprietor Christian Hansen. The hotel was taken over by Annie Hansen in 1920, and pulled down and rebuilt in 1926.

In 1944 the hotel was sold to new owners, but it wasn't until 1955 that a liquor licence was granted, and the pub was born as the New Oban Hotel. In 1968, it was renamed the South Sea Hotel, and the lounge bar was added.

The premises seem disproportionately large for such a small community, but on a Sunday evening you'd be hard pressed to get a seat for the weekly pub quiz, which packs in the punters. Latecomers resort to perching around the pool table or piano.

The many old photos on the walls display the island's fishing history, as well as the 10-year period when it operated a ship repair facility for a Norwegian whaling company. More lighthearted pictures include the visit of a sea lion, which managed to find its way to the ladies' bathroom.

The country's southernmost hotel is packed with artefacts that attest to its provision of haircuts and dental work, as well as a resting place for the weary providing refreshments and entertainment. It's hard to single out the star of this fascinating pub, but the view from the lounge window looking out to the boats in the bay must surely entice many to stay for just one more round.

THE LUMSDEN HOTEL

6 Diana St Lumsden, Junction of SH 6 and SH 94
Ph: 03 248 7817
Web: www. thelumsdenhotel.co.nz
Built: 1875
Food: For a country pub the Lumsden has a very eclectic menu, ranging from burgers and pizzas through to curries and dumplings.
Accommodation: A mixture of ensuite and shared bathrooms.

In a town of less than 500 people, the Lumsden Hotel is by far the oldest and most substantial building in the district. Originally called the Lumsden Railway Hotel, the name reflected the importance of this small town on the banks of the Oreti River as a busy railway junction. Not only was it a railway junction, but Lumsden was an important road junction as well, boasting a huge sale yards for farmers bringing their stock to market from all over northern Southland.

The baby farmer Minnie Dean stayed in the hotel on her way to Gore with her infamous hatbox in hand.

With lines running both north and south, and west and west, the town fell into decline when the railways closed down one after another. However, given its location at the junction of major highways the recent boom in tourism, revived the town's fortunes, especially with cyclists and trout fishers. The area around the old railway station has been turned into a very popular parking spot for camper vans.

More importantly, the owners stepped up to meet the challenge renovating the rooms, expanding the main bar, creating a great pub menu and providing live music. Today the Lumsden Hotel is humming, and the busy establishment recalls the hotels of the past where anything of any importance happens in the pub.

INDEX

PHOTO CREDITS

Page 17 Duke of Marlborough Hotel
Page 21 historic Towai Hotel
Page 22 historic Kamo Hotel
Page 26 historic Parua Bay Hotel
Page 30 historic Northern Wairoa Hotel
Pages 22,23 Paparoa Hotel
Page 34 The Mangawhai Tavern – Mark Grimmer
Pages 44,45 Riverhead Tavern
Pags 47, 48 Northcote Tavern
Page 99 The Royal Oak Hotel – Kaye Bunn
Pages 109,110 Waikino Hotel
Page 113 The Talisman Hotel – Danielle Watts
Page 130, Masonic Hotel
Page 132, Susan Holmes
Page 143, Historic Whangamomana Hotel
Pages 166,167,170, 171, Greytown Hotel
Pages 181,182 Thistle Inn
Page 231 Theatre Royal Hotel
Page 291 Carey's Bay Hotel
Page 302, 303 The Rope and Twine – Rope and Twine
Pages 330, 331 The Cardrona Hotel
Page 344 Riverton Heritage Society
Pages 349,350, 352, 354 Jo Hammer

All other images author's own.

Things change and mistakes happen.

In a book crammed with information it is inevitable that things never stay the same as pubs close, change ownership or are renovated. Mistakes also happen despite all the checking, including the inevitable typos and plain old-fashioned carelessness.

When books are reprinted there is usually the opportunity to make text corrections, so it is helpful to hear from anyone who spots a mistake or is aware of changes. Email me at changesandmistakes@gmail.com

First published in 2018 by New Holland Publishers
This edition published by New Holland Publishers in 2021
Sydney • Auckland

Level 1, 178 Fox Valley Road, Wahroonga, 2076, NSW, Australia
5/39 Woodside Ave, Northcote, Auckland 0627, New Zealand

newhollandpublishers.com

Copyright © 2021 New Holland Publishers
Copyright © 2021 in text: Peter Janssen
Copyright © 2021 in images: Peter Janssen and others as stated on Picture Credits page.

All rights reserved. No part of this publication may be reproduced, stored in a retrieval system or transmitted, in any form or by any means, electronic, mechanical, photocopying, recording or otherwise, without the prior written permission of the publishers and copyright holders.

A catalogue record for this book is available from the National Library of New Zealand.

ISBN 9781869665524

Group Managing Director: Fiona Schultz
Publisher: David Brash
Project Editor: Duncan Perkinson
Designer: Sara Lindberg
Production Director: Arlene Gippert
Printed in China

10 9 8 7 6 5 4 3 2 1

Keep up with New Holland Publishers on Facebook
facebook.com/NewHollandPublishers